Collins

AQA GCSE 9-1

Chemistry

Chemistry

AQA
GCSE 9-1

Workbook

Emma Poole and Gemma Young

Revision Tips

Rethink Revision

Have you ever taken part in a quiz and thought *'I know this!'* but, despite frantically racking your brain, you just couldn't come up with the answer?

It's very frustrating when this happens but, in a fun situation, it doesn't really matter. However, in your GCSE exams, it will be essential that you can recall the relevant information quickly when you need to.

Most students think that revision is about making sure you **know** stuff. Of course, this is important, but it is also about becoming confident that you can **retain** that *stuff* over time and **recall** it quickly when needed.

Revision That Really Works

Experts have discovered that there are two techniques that help with all of these things and consistently produce better results in exams compared to other revision techniques.

Applying these techniques to your GCSE revision will ensure you get better results in your exams and will have all the relevant knowledge at your fingertips when you start studying for further qualifications, like AS and A Levels, or begin work.

It really isn't rocket science either – you simply need to:

- **test yourself** on each topic as many times as possible
- **leave a gap** between the test sessions.

Three Essential Revision Tips

1. **Use Your Time Wisely**

   - Allow yourself plenty of time.
   - Try to start revising at least six months before your exams – it's more effective and less stressful.
   - Your revision time is precious so use it wisely – using the techniques described on this page will ensure you revise effectively and efficiently and get the best results.
   - Don't waste time re-reading the same information over and over again – it's time-consuming and not effective!

2. **Make a Plan**

   - Identify all the topics you need to revise.
   - Plan at least five sessions for each topic.
   - One hour should be ample time to test yourself on the key ideas for a topic.
   - Spread out the practice sessions for each topic – the optimum time to leave between each session is about one month but, if this isn't possible, just make the gaps as big as realistically possible.

3. **Test Yourself**

   - Methods for testing yourself include: quizzes, practice questions, flashcards, past papers, explaining a topic to someone else, etc.
   - Don't worry if you get an answer wrong – provided you check what the correct answer is, you are more likely to get the same or similar questions right in future!

Visit our website for more information about the benefits of these techniques and for further guidance on how to plan ahead and make them work for you.

www.collins.co.uk/collinsGCSErevision

Contents

Atoms, Elements, Compounds and Mixtures

1 A student heated a piece of copper in air.
The word equation for the reaction is:

copper + oxygen → copper(II) oxide

a) Which equation correctly represents the reaction?
Tick **one** box.

$Cu + O → CuO$ ☐

$2Cu + 2O → 2CuO$ ☐

$2Cu + O_2 → 2CuO$ ☐

$Cu_2 + O_2 → 2CuO$ ☐ [1]

b) The mass of the copper before heating was 15.6g.
The mass of copper oxide produced was 18.9g.

Calculate the mass of oxygen that was used in the reaction.

Answer: _____ g [1]

c) What was the resolution of the balance the student used to measure the masses?

Answer: _____ g [1]

2 A student was asked to produce pure water from salt solution.

a) Describe how they would do
this using the equipment in **Figure 1**.

Figure 1

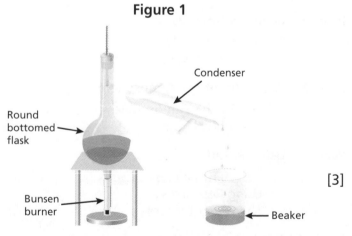

_____

_____

_____

_____

_____ [3]

b) State **one** hazard when carrying out
this procedure.

_____ [1]

Total Marks _____ / 7

Atoms and the Periodic Table

1 Early models of atoms showed them as tiny spheres that could not be divided into simpler substances.

In 1897, Thompson discovered that atoms contained small negatively charged particles. He proposed a new model shown in **Figure 1.**

Figure 1

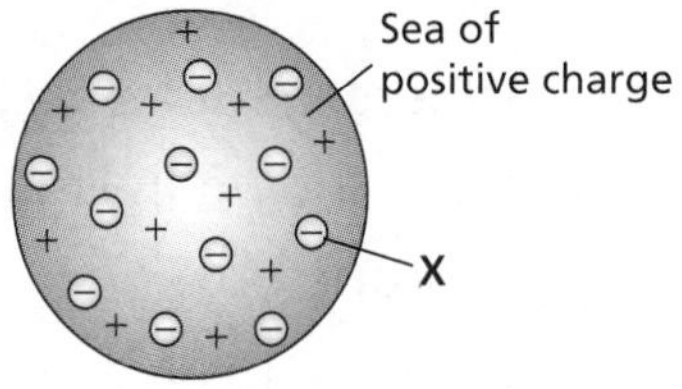

a) Why did the model of the atom have to change?

....

....

.... [2]

b) Name the particle labelled **X**.

Answer: .... [1]

2 In 1909, Geiger and Marsden bombarded a thin sheet of gold with positively charged alpha particles. They found that most passed through, but some were deflected back.

a) Explain why this result was unexpected.

....

.... [1]

b) Explain why they would have repeated their experiment several times.

....

....

.... [2]

c) Describe the new model of the atom that resulted from this experiment.

....

....

....

.... [3]

Total Marks .... / 9

The Periodic Table

1   An unknown element has the electronic configuration 2,8,8,7.

Where would it be found in the periodic table shown in **Figure 1**?
Tick **one** box.

A ☐   B ☐

C ☐   D ☐

Figure 1

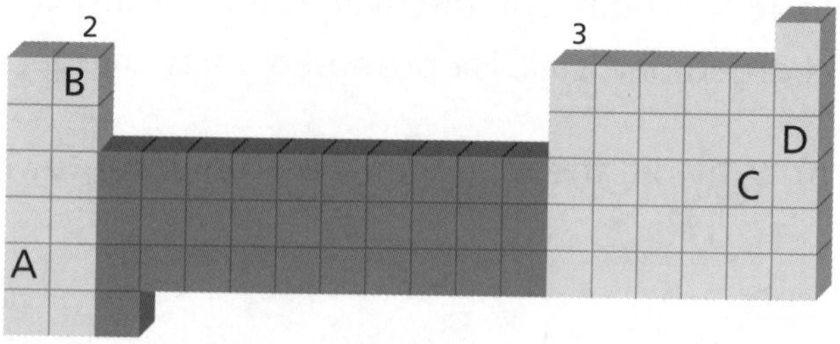

[1]

2   **Table 1** shows some data on the physical properties of elements.

Table 1

Physical Property	Element W	Element X	Element Y	Element Z
Melting Point (°C)	−38.82	−189.34	180.5	1538
Density (g/cm³)	13.53	1.40	0.53	7.87
Conductor of Electricity?	Yes	No	Yes	Yes

a) Which element, **W, X, Y** or **Z**, is a non-metal?
   Give a reason for your answer.

   ....

   .... [2]

b) Which element, **W, X, Y** or **Z**, is mercury?
   Give a reason for your answer.

   ....

   ....

   .... [3]

c) One of the elements is a Group 1 metal.
   Compare the physical and chemical properties of Group 1 metals and transition metals.

   ....

   ....

   .... [3]

Total Marks .... / 9

States of Matter

1 A student burns magnesium.

It reacts with oxygen in the air to form a white powder called magnesium oxide.

a) Add the missing state symbols to the equation for the reaction.

$2Mg(s) + O_2(\underline{\quad}) \rightarrow 2MgO(\underline{\quad})$ [2]

Table 1 contains some information about the melting and boiling points of the substances involved in the reaction.

Table 1

	Magnesium	Oxygen	Magnesium Oxide
Melting Point (°C)	650	−219	2830
Boiling Point (°C)	1091	−183	3600

b) State the temperature at which magnesium would change from a solid into a liquid.

Answer: .... °C [1]

c) State the temperature that oxygen gas would have to be cooled to in order for it to condense.

Answer: .... °C [1]

d) Explain, in terms of bonding, the difference in boiling points between oxygen and magnesium oxide.

....

....

....

....

....

....

....

....

.... [6]

Total Marks .... / 10

Ionic Compounds

1 A student investigated the properties of some different compounds.

a) Which of the following compounds contain ionic bonds?
   Tick **two** boxes.

   water (H_2O) ☐

   calcium chloride ($CaCl_2$) ☐

   glucose ($C_6H_{12}O_6$) ☐

   sodium carbonate (Na_2CO_3) ☐

   hydrogen chloride (HCl) ☐

   [2]

b) The student discovered that the ionic compounds would not conduct electricity when solid but they would when dissolved in water.

   Explain why.

   ....

   ....

   ....

   [3]

2 **Figure 1** shows the outer electrons in an atom of the Group 2 element magnesium and in an atom of the Group 7 element bromine.
   Magnesium forms an ionic compound with bromine.

   Describe what happens when **one** atom of magnesium reacts with **two** atoms of bromine.
   Give your answer in terms of electron transfer.
   Give the formulae of the ions formed.

   Figure 1

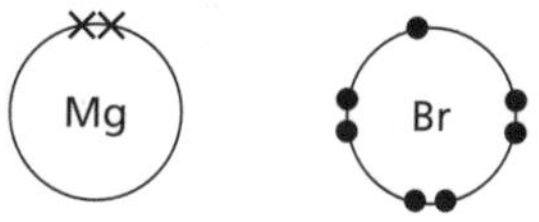

   ....

   ....

   ....

   ....

   ....

   ....

   [5]

Total Marks .... / 10

Metals

1 **Figure 1** shows the bonding in the metal copper.

Figure 1

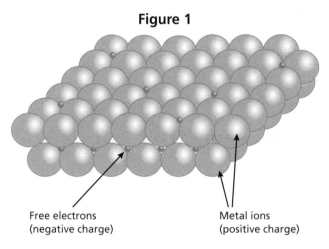

Free electrons
(negative charge)

Metal ions
(positive charge)

Copper is useful as a material for making saucepans.
This is because it has the following properties:

- high melting point
- good thermal conductor
- malleable (can be easily shaped).

Explain, in terms of its metallic bonding, why copper has these properties.

....

....

....

....

....

....

....

.... **[6]**

Total Marks .... / 6

Covalent Compounds

1 Fluorine and bromine are elements found in Group 7 of the periodic table.
At room temperature fluorine is a gas and bromine is a liquid.

Why, at room temperature, is fluorine a gas and bromine a liquid?
Tick **one** box.

The covalent bonds between bromine are stronger. ☐

Bromine has a giant covalent structure and fluorine is a simple molecule. ☐

The forces between bromine molecules are stronger. ☐

Fluorine contains fewer molecules than bromine. ☐ [1]

2 Bromine reacts with hydrogen to form hydrogen bromide.

Figure 1

a) Complete the dot and cross diagram in **Figure 1** to show
the covalent bonding in a molecule of hydrogen bromide.

Show the outer shell electrons only.

[2]

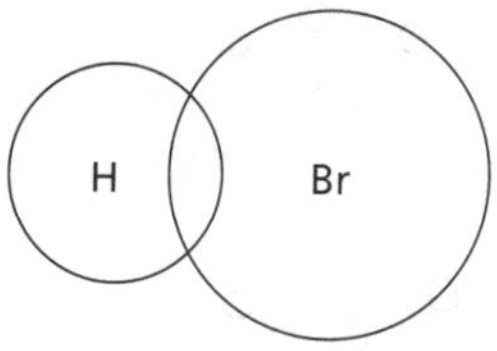

b) State the formula for a molecule of hydrogen bromide.

Answer: _____ [1]

3 Diamond has a giant covalent structure made up of carbon atoms.
It has a high melting point and does not conduct electricity when molten.

Draw **one** line from each property to the explanation of that property.

Property	Explanation of Property
	Strong covalent bonds between many carbon atoms
High melting point	Atoms are free to move
	Weak bonds between carbon atoms
Does not conduct electricity when molten	There are no charged particles that are free to move
	Carbon atoms are in a regular arrangement

[2]

Total Marks _____ / 6

Special Materials

1 Zinc oxide is used in sun creams. Its particles reflect UV light waves.

a) In the past, particles of zinc oxide with a diameter of 1×10^{-6}m were used in sun cream.
Now, nanoparticles of a diameter of 1×10^{-8}m are used.

Calculate how many orders of magnitude the diameters of the particles has been reduced by.

Answer: .... [1]

b) Explain how reducing the size of the zinc oxide particles increases the effectiveness
of the sun cream.

....

....

.... [3]

2 Nanoparticles have a diameter of between 1 and 100nm (1nm = 0.000 000 001m).
A sun cream manufacturer claims that its product contains no nanoparticles.
The average diameter of the particles it contains is 0.000 000 055m.

a) Express this number in standard form. Answer: .... m [1]

b) Is the sun cream manufacturer's claim correct? Give a reason for your answer.

....

.... [2]

3 A scientific study was carried out during which 10 volunteers applied sun cream containing
zinc oxide nanoparticles twice a day.
After 5 days, less than 0.01% of the nanoparticles had entered the bloodstream.
The scientists concluded that there is no danger from zinc oxide nanoparticles in sun cream.

Describe what extra information you would need to know before you can decide if there is
a danger from zinc oxide nanoparticles in sun cream.

....

....

....

.... [3]

Total Marks .... / 10

Conservation of Mass

1 A student was asked to carry out the reaction shown in the word equation:

zinc + hydrochloric acid ➜ zinc chloride + hydrogen

a) What is the ionic equation for the reaction?
Tick **one** box.

$Zn(s) + 2HCl(aq) ➜ ZnCl_2(aq) + H_2(g)$ ☐

$Zn^{2+}(aq) + 2Cl^-(aq) ➜ ZnCl_2(aq)$ ☐

$Zn(s) + 2H^+(aq) ➜ Zn^{2+}(aq) + H_2(g)$ ☐

$Zn(s) + 2Cl^-(aq) ➜ ZnCl_2(aq)$ ☐ [1]

b) The student plans to use the equipment in **Figure 1**.
The teacher tells the student not to use the bung.

Explain why.

....

....

....

....

[2]

Figure 1

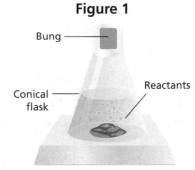

Bung

Conical flask

Reactants

c) The student carries out the reaction on a balance, as shown in **Figure 2**.

Figure 2

Explain what happens to the mass reading during the reaction.

....

....

....

....

[3]

Total Marks .... / 6

Amount of Substance

1 **Figure 1** shows a cube of pure silver with a side length of 2cm.

Figure 1

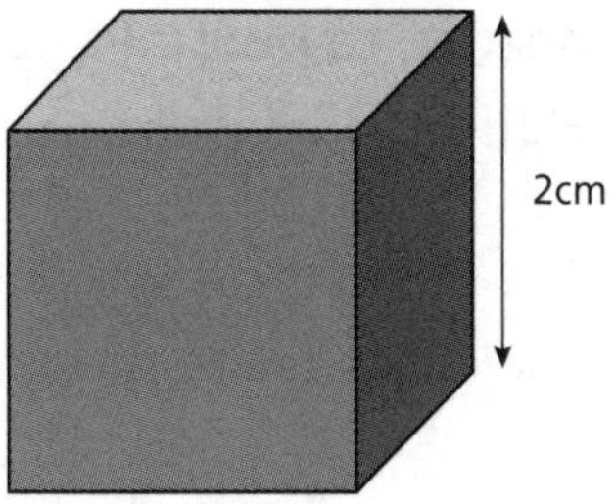

2cm

a) Calculate the volume of the cube.

Answer: _____ cm³ [1]

b) The density of silver is 10.49g/cm³.

Use the formula density = $\frac{mass}{volume}$ to calculate the mass of the silver cube to 2 decimal places.

Answer: _____ g [2]

c) Calculate how many moles of silver are in the cube to 2 decimal places.
(Relative atomic mass, A_r, of silver = 108)

Answer: _____ moles [2]

d) There are 6.02×10^{23} atoms in one mole of silver.

Which of the following also contains 6.02×10^{23} atoms?
(Relative atomic masses, A_r: C = 12, O = 16)
Tick **two** boxes.

1 mole of oxygen (O_2) ☐

0.5 mole of oxygen (O_2) ☐

12g of carbon (C) ☐

6g of carbon (C) ☐ [2]

Total Marks _____ / 7

Titration

1 A student carried out a titration to find out the volume of 0.100mol/dm³ hydrochloric acid needed to neutralise 25.0cm³ of sodium hydroxide of unknown concentration.
Figure 1 shows the apparatus they used.

The student carried out four titrations.
Their results are shown in **Table 1**.

Figure 1

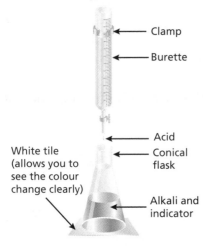

White tile (allows you to see the colour change clearly)

Clamp
Burette
Acid
Conical flask
Alkali and indicator

Table 1

Titration	1	2	3	4
Volume of Acid Needed to Neutralise the Alkali (cm³)	29.65	27.15	27.05	26.95

a) The result for Titration 1 is anomalous.

Suggest what may have happened to cause this anomalous result.

....

....

.... [1]

b) What volume of acid was needed to neutralise the alkali?
Show how you arrived at your answer.

Answer: .... cm³ [2]

c) The equation for the reaction is:

HCl + NaOH → NaCl + H$_2$O

Calculate the concentration of the sodium hydroxide.
Give your answer to three significant figures.

Answer: .... mol/dm³ [5]

Total Marks .... / 8

Percentage Yield and Atom Economy

1. A student prepared magnesium oxide using the method shown in **Figure 1**.

Figure 1

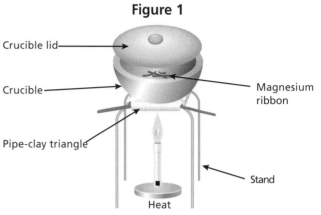

The equation for the reaction is:

$2Mg(s) + O_2(g) \rightarrow 2MgO(s)$

a) The student used 3.6g of magnesium ribbon.

Calculate the theoretical yield of magnesium oxide.
(Relative atomic masses, A_r: O = 16, Mg = 24)

Answer: .... g   [3]

b) The student produced less magnesium oxide than the theoretical yield.

Suggest **one** reason why.

....

.... [1]

c) The atom economy of this reaction is 100%.

Explain why.

....

.... [1]

Total Marks .... / 5

Reactivity of Metals

1   This question is about how metals are extracted from their ores.
    Figure 1 shows the reactivity series of metals.

Figure 1

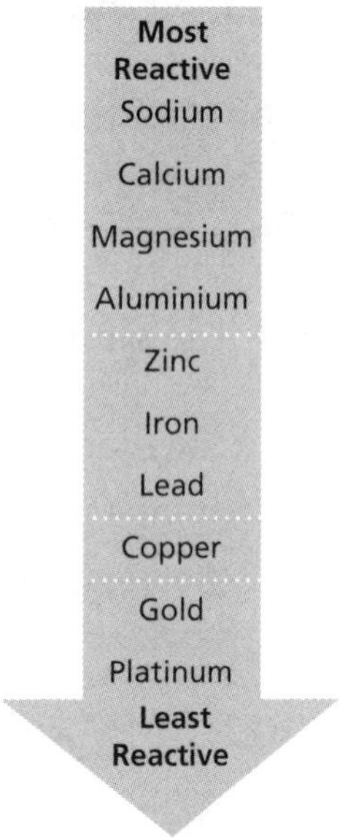

Most
Reactive

Sodium

Calcium

Magnesium

Aluminium

Zinc

Iron

Lead

Copper

Gold

Platinum

Least
Reactive

a) Zinc can be found naturally as the compound zinc(II) oxide.

Use the information in **Figure 1** to decide which of these metals can be
used to displace zinc from zinc(II) oxide.
Tick **two** boxes.

magnesium   ☐   iron   ☐

copper   ☐   sodium   ☐   [2]

b) In reality, carbon is used to extract zinc from zinc(II) oxide.
The equation for the reaction is:

zinc(II) oxide + carbon → zinc + carbon monoxide

i) State the substance that is oxidised during the reaction.

Answer: _____ [1]

ii) State the substance that is reduced during the reaction.

Answer: _____ [1]

2   A student reacted zinc with a solution of copper chloride:

$Zn + CuCl_2 \rightarrow ZnCl_2 + Cu$

Draw **one** line from each change that takes place in this reaction to the correct
half equation.

Change	Half Equation
	$Cu \rightarrow Cu^{2+} + 2e^-$
Oxidation	
	$Zn \rightarrow Zn^{2+} + 2e^-$
	$Zn^{2+} + 2e^- \rightarrow Zn$
Reduction	$Zn^{2-} \rightarrow 2e^- + Zn$
	$Cu^{2+} + 2e^- \rightarrow Cu$

[2]

Total Marks _____ / 6

The pH Scale and Salts

1 Universal indicator was added to a sample of an unknown solution.
The universal indicator turned orange.

What is the pH value of the solution?
Tick **one** box.

1 ☐   7 ☐

4 ☐   10 ☐   [1]

2 A student was asked to prepare pure, dry crystals of a soluble salt using insoluble copper(II) oxide and hydrochloric acid.
First, the student measured out 25cm³ of acid into a conical flask.

a) Describe how the student should complete the preparation of the salt.

....

....

....

....

....

....

....

....

....   [4]

b) State **one** safety precaution that the student should take during the preparation.

....

....   [1]

c) Name the salt produced.

Answer: ....   [1]

Total Marks .... / 7

Electrolysis

1 Aluminium is extracted from its ore, aluminium oxide, using electrolysis, as shown in **Figure 1**.

Figure 1

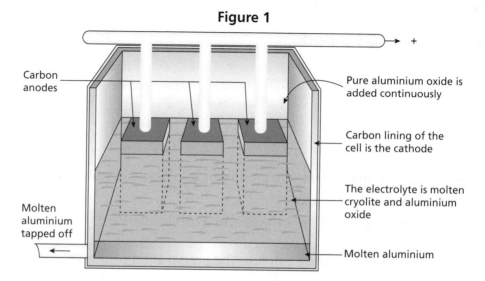

a) Explain why aluminium cannot be extracted from aluminium oxide using reduction with carbon.

....

.... [1]

b) Balance the half equation for the reaction that occurs at the carbon anodes.

.... $O^{2-} \rightarrow$ .... $e^- + O_2$ [2]

c) Explain why the extraction of aluminium from aluminium oxide is an expensive process and describe the methods used by manufacturers to reduce the cost.

....

....

....

....

....

....

....

....

.... [3]

Total Marks .... / 6

Exothermic and Endothermic Reactions

1 A student carried out an investigation into how the reactivity of metals affects how exothermic or endothermic their reaction with dilute hydrochloric acid is.

The student used the apparatus shown in **Figure 1**.

The student's results are shown in **Table 1**.

Figure 1

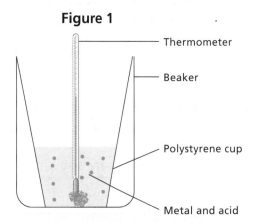

Thermometer

Beaker

Polystyrene cup

Metal and acid

Table 1

Metal	Temperature at Start (°C)	Highest Temperature Reached (°C)
Zinc	21.0	30.1
Copper	21.2	21.3
Magnesium	21.4	82.6
Iron	21.4	26.0

a) Describe the function of the polystyrene cup.

....

....

.... [2]

b) State **two** control variables the student should have used in this investigation.

....

.... [2]

c) The order of reactivity of these metals from highest to lowest is: magnesium, zinc, iron, copper.

Write a conclusion which answers the original question that the student was investigating.

....

....

.... [2]

Total Marks .... / 6

Fuel Cells

1 A student investigated simple cells using the apparatus shown in **Figure** 1.

- If Metal 2 is more reactive than copper, then the voltage measured is positive.

- If copper is more reactive than Metal 2, then the voltage measured is negative.

- The bigger the difference in reactivity of the two metals, the larger the voltage produced.

The student's results are shown in **Table 1**.

Figure 1

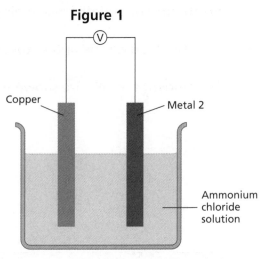

Table 1

Metal 2	Voltage
A	−0.8 V
B	1.2 V
C	0.8 V
D	−0.4 V

a) A cell containing two electrodes of the same metal would not be useful.

Explain why.

....

.... [1]

b) Look at the results in **Table 1**.

Which one of the metals used was the least reactive?
Give a reason for your answer.

....

.... [2]

c) Explain how you could produce a battery with a voltage of 6.0V using copper and Metal **B**.

....

....

....

.... [2]

Total Marks .... / 5

Rate of Reaction

1 When hydrochloric acid reacts with sodium thiosulfate one of the products is sulfur, which is insoluble.

A student carried out an investigation into the following hypothesis:

As the concentration of acid increases, the rate of the reaction will increase.

Figure 1

The student added sodium thiosulfate to dilute hydrochloric acid of concentration 0.25mol/dm³ in a conical flask.
The conical flask was placed on a cross, as shown in **Figure 1.**
The student timed how long it took before they could no longer see the cross.

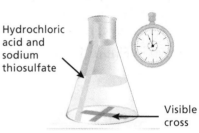

a) Describe what the student should do next in order to investigate the hypothesis. You should include a suitable range for the independent variable in your answer.

....

....

....

.... **[2]**

b) State **one** safety precaution the student should take.

.... **[1]**

c) Use collision theory to write a prediction for what will happen if the hypothesis is correct.

....

....

....

....

.... **[4]**

Total Marks .... / 7

Reversible Reactions

1 This question is about the reaction between ammonia and hydrogen chloride.

The equation for the reaction is:

$$NH_3(g) + HCl(g) \rightleftharpoons NH_4Cl(s)$$

The reaction can be carried out using the apparatus shown in **Figure 1**.

Figure 1

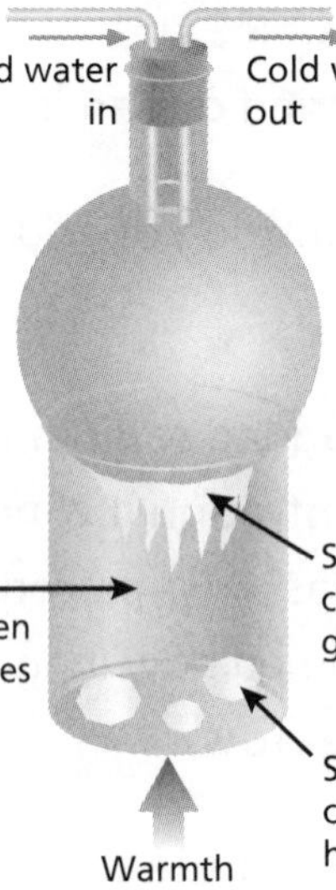

Cold water in → ← Cold water out

Ammonia and hydrogen chloride gases

Solid ammonium chloride formed by gases recombining

Solid ammonium chloride being heated

Warmth

a) What is meant by the symbol $\rightleftharpoons$ in the equation?

.... [1]

b) Which reaction, the forward reaction or the reverse reaction, is exothermic?
Give a reason for your answer.

....

....

.... [3]

c) The reaction taking place in **Figure 1** is at equilibrium.

What does this mean?
Tick **two** boxes.

Only ammonium chloride is being produced. ☐

The forward and reverse reactions are taking place at the same rate. ☐

The amounts of reactants and products are constant. ☐

The reaction has completed. ☐ [2]

d) More ammonia is added into the mixture.

Predict what will happen.

....

....

.... [2]

Total Marks .... / 8

Alkanes

1 Fractional distillation is used to separate crude oil into useful mixtures called fractions.
It takes place in a column, as shown in **Figure 1**.

a) The molecules found in crude oil are mostly hydrocarbons.

What is a hydrocarbon?

....

....

....

[2]

Figure 1

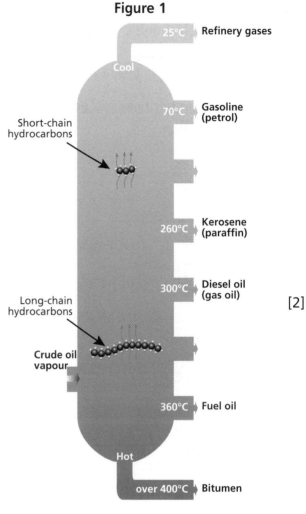

b) This is what takes place inside the column:

1. Crude oil is heated until it forms a vapour.
2. The vapour rises up the tower.

Describe what happens next in order for the fractions to form.

....

....

....

....

....

....

[2]

2 Methane (CH_4) is the name of a hydrocarbon found in refinery gas.

Complete the balanced symbol equation for the complete combustion of methane.

$CH_4 + 2$ .... $\rightarrow CO_2 +$ .... H_2O

[2]

Total Marks .... / 6

Alkenes

1 Hydrocarbon molecules can be cracked to form molecules with shorter chains.
The equation shows the cracking of $C_{20}H_{42}$.

$$C_{20}H_{42} \rightarrow C_8H_{18} + \boxed{}\, C_5H_{10} + C_2H_4$$

a) What number needs to go in the box to balance the equation?
Tick **one** box.

1 ☐

2 ☐

3 ☐

4 ☐ [1]

b) Which products are alkenes?
Tick **one** box.

C_8H_{18} and C_2H_4 ☐

C_5H_{10} and C_2H_4 ☐

C_2H_4 only ☐

C_8H_{18}, C_5H_{10} and C_2H_4 ☐ [1]

2 A student is given a test tube of colourless liquid hydrocarbon.

Describe a test the student could carry out to find out if the liquid is an alkane or an alkene.
You should state the chemical used for the test and the results of the test for both an alkane and an alkene.

....

....

....

....

....

[3]

Total Marks .... / 5

Organic Compounds

1 A student carried out some experiments using an alcohol.
Its structure is shown in **Figure 1**.

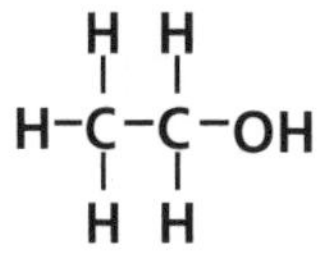

a) Circle the functional group on the diagram in **Figure 1**. [1]

Figure 1

$$H-\overset{\overset{\displaystyle H}{|}}{\underset{\underset{\displaystyle H}{|}}{C}}-\overset{\overset{\displaystyle H}{|}}{\underset{\underset{\displaystyle H}{|}}{C}}-OH$$

b) Name the alcohol in **Figure 1**.

Answer: .... [1]

c) For each of the experiments below, describe what the student would observe and why.

i) Dissolving the alcohol in water and testing the solution with universal indicator.

Observation:

....

Reason:

....

....

.... [2]

ii) Adding sodium to the alcohol.

Observation:

....

Reason:

....

....

.... [2]

d) The student was asked to make an ester.

State the organic substance that the student needed to react the alcohol with to produce an ester.

Answer: .... [1]

Total Marks .... / 7

Polymerisation

1 Propene can undergo a polymerisation reaction, as shown in **Figure 1**.

Figure 1

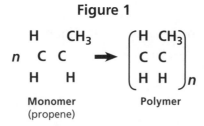

Monomer
(propene)

Polymer

a) Draw the bonds to complete the equation for the reaction shown in **Figure 1**. [3]

b) Name the polymer produced in this reaction.

Answer: .... [1]

2 Polymers can be thermosoftening or thermosetting.

Figure 2 shows the structure of each type of polymer.

Figure 2

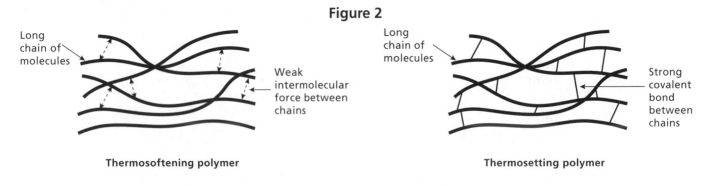

Use the diagrams in **Figure 2** to explain why thermosoftening plastics melt when they are heated but thermosetting plastics do not melt. [4]

....

....

....

....

....

Total Marks .... / 8

Chemical Analysis

1 A student was asked to investigate five different inks using chromatography.
Figure 1 shows the apparatus they needed to use.
The student set up the apparatus correctly and left it for several minutes.
Figure 2 shows their results.

Figure 1

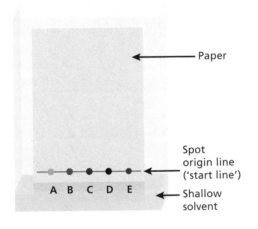

Figure 2

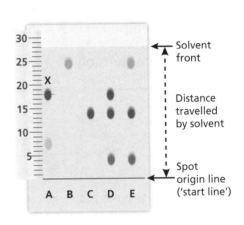

a) Which part of the apparatus is the stationary phase?

Answer: _____ [1]

b) The student was not sure whether to use a pen or pencil to draw the origin line.

State which they should choose. Give a reason for your answer.

_____

_____ [2]

c) Which **two** inks are pure? Give a reason for your answer.

_____

_____ [2]

d) Calculate the R_f value of **X**.
Give your answer to 2 decimal places.

Answer: _____ [3]

Total Marks _____ / 8

Identifying Substances

1 A student was asked to identify an unknown ionic compound.
The student carried out a series of chemical tests.
The first test was a flame test.
They used this method:

1. Heat and then dip a nichrome wire in concentrated hydrochloric acid.
2. Dip the wire in the compound.
3. Hold the compound in a Bunsen flame and observe the colour of the flame.

a) Describe the function of step 1.

....

....

.... [2]

Table 1 shows the results.

Table 1

Test	Observations
Flame test	A yellow flame
Mixing with silver nitrate and a few drops of dilute nitric acid	A white precipitate forms

b) Suggest the name of the unknown compound.
   Give reasons for your answer.

....

....

....

....

.... [4]

c) The compound can also be identified using instrumental methods.

   State **two** advantages of using instrumental methods instead of the chemical tests used by the student.

....

....

.... [2]

Total Marks .... / 8

The Earth's Atmosphere

1 **Table 1** shows some of the gases that are in the Earth's atmosphere today.

Which letter, **A**, **B**, **C** or **D**, represents the correct proportions?
Tick **one** box.

Table 1

	Oxygen	Nitrogen	Carbon Dioxide
A	80%	20%	0.04%
B	0.04%	80%	20%
C	20%	80%	0.04%
D	20%	0.04%	80%

A ☐

B ☐

C ☐

D ☐

[1]

2 The percentage of water vapour in the atmosphere can vary.
4.2dm³ of air contains 0.05dm³ of water vapour.

Calculate the percentage of water vapour in the air.
Give your answer to 2 significant figures.

Answer: .... %   [2]

3 One theory for how the Earth's early atmosphere was formed is that gases were released by volcanoes.
Scientists have recently proposed a new theory: that the early atmosphere was formed by comets hitting the Earth.

a) What would the scientists need for this new theory to be accepted?

....

.... [2]

b) Explain why we cannot be sure if either theory is correct.

....

....

....

.... [3]

Total Marks .... / 8

Greenhouse Gases

1 Many scientists believe that human activities are causing the mean global temperature of the Earth to increase.

They think that this is because of an increase in the amounts of greenhouse gases in the atmosphere.

Water vapour is an example of a greenhouse gas.

a) Name one other greenhouse gas and state how human activity has increased its amount in the atmosphere.

....

....

....   [2]

In 2000, computer models were used to predict how the mean global temperature might change in the future.

Figure 1 shows the results. Each line shows the predictions made using a different model.

Figure 1

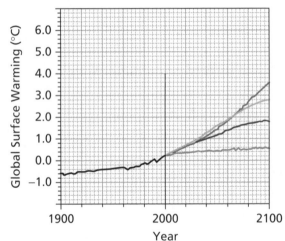

b) Calculate the range of global surface warming as predicted for 2100 by the different models.

From: ....   To: ....   [2]

c) Explain why it is difficult to produce models to predict future climate change.

....

....

....   [2]

Total Marks .... / 6

Earth's Resources

1 In the UK, potable water is produced from an unpolluted source of fresh water.
Potable water contains low levels of dissolved substances.

a) What is potable water?

.... [1]

b) Explain why potable water cannot be called pure in the chemical sense.

....

....

....

.... [2]

The stages of producing potable water from fresh water are:

1. Pass the water through filter beds to remove any solids.
2. Sterilise the water to kill microorganisms.

c) Give **one** way of sterilising the water.

.... [1]

In other parts of the world, sea water is used as a source of potable water.
To produce potable water from sea water a process called distillation is used.

d) Explain why distillation is used.

....

.... [1]

e) Explain why producing potable water from sea water is more expensive than producing
it from fresh water sources.

....

....

....

.... [2]

Total Marks .... / 7

Using Resources

1 Shopping bags can be made out of paper or plastic.

Table 1 is part of a LCA (life cycle assessment) comparing these two materials.

Table 1

	Paper Bag	Plastic Bag
Raw Materials	Wood pulp	Crude oil
Manufacture	• Wood pulp is added to water (up to 100 times the mass of the pulp) and mixed. • Clay, chalk or titanium oxide is added. • The mixture is squeezed and heated to remove the water.	• Crude oil is heated to 360°C during fractional distillation. • A fraction is cracked at 850°C to produce alkenes. • Polymerisation of alkenes at 150°C.
Transport	• Average mass = 55g • Seven trucks needed to transport two million bags.	• Average mass = 7g • One truck needed to transport two million bags.
Use During Lifetime	• Not normally reused.	• Can be reused many times.
Disposal at the End of Life	• Taken to landfill (biodegradable). • Can be incinerated (burned). • Can be recycled.	• Taken to landfill (not biodegradable). • Can be incinerated (burned). • Difficult to recycle.

Use the information in **Table 1** to compare the **advantages** and **disadvantages** of both types of bag.

[6]

Total Marks _____ / 6

The Haber Process

1 **Figure 1** shows how ammonia is produced using the Haber process.

Figure 1

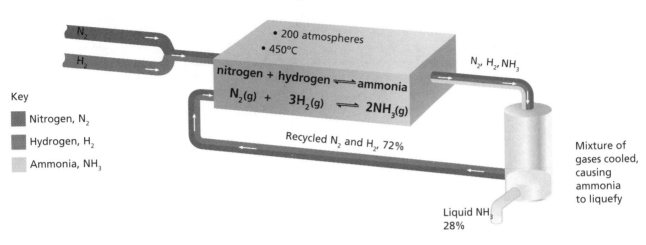

a) During the process hydrogen, nitrogen and iron are added into a reaction chamber.

What is the function of the iron?

....

.... [2]

b) Explain why the ammonia gas is liquefied immediately after it has formed.

....

.... [2]

2 Ammonia is used to make fertilisers.
It supplies the nitrogen (N) in NPK fertilisers.

a) What do the P and K stand for in NPK fertilisers?

P: .... K: .... [2]

b) A fertiliser contains 24% nitrogen.

Calculate how much nitrogen is present in 20kg of the fertiliser.

Answer: .... kg [2]

Total Marks .... / 8

Notes

Collins

GCSE
CHEMISTRY
Paper 1 Higher Tier

Materials

Time allowed: 1 hour 45 minutes

For this paper you must have:

- a ruler
- a calculator
- the periodic table (see page 72).

Instructions

- Answer **all** questions in the spaces provided.
- Do all rough work on the page. Cross through any work you do not want to be marked.

Information

- There are **100** marks available on this paper.
- The marks for each question are shown in brackets.
- You are expected to use a calculator where appropriate.
- You are reminded of the need for good English and clear presentation in your answers.

Advice

- In all calculations, show clearly how you work out your answer.

Practice Exam Paper 1

01 This question is about the atomic model.

Figure 1 shows a model of a helium atom.

Figure 1

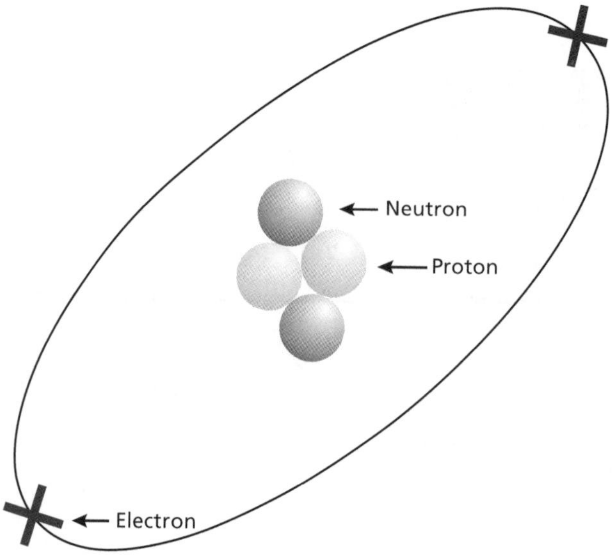

01.1 What are the relative electric charges on the particles in an atom?

Tick **one** box.

Proton	Neutron	Electron	
0	−1	+1	☐
+1	0	−1	☐
−1	0	0	☐
+1	+1	−1	☐

[1 mark]

01.2 A helium atom has an overall neutral charge.

State why.

....

.... **[1 mark]**

01.3 What is the mass number and atomic number of helium?

Tick **one** box.

Mass Number	Atomic Number		
2	2	☐	
6	2	☐	
6	4	☐	
4	2	☐	[1 mark]

01.4 Why is helium an unreactive element?

Tick **one** box.

It has an equal number of protons and neutrons. ☐

Elements with two electrons in their outer shell are unreactive. ☐

It is a gas at room temperature and pressure. ☐

It has a full outer shell of electrons. ☐ [1 mark]

01.5 An isotope of helium has only one neutron in its atoms.

Which statements about how an atom of this isotope compares to the atom in **Figure 1** are true?

Tick **two** boxes.

It has the same atomic number. ☐

It has a higher mass. ☐

It has a different atomic number. ☐

It has a different mass number. ☐

It has the same mass number. ☐ [2 marks]

Turn over for the next question

02   Iron is found in the Earth as the compound iron oxide (Fe_2O_3).

    02.1 How many atoms are in one molecule of Fe_2O_3?

         Answer: .... **[1 mark]**

    Iron is extracted from iron(III) oxide using carbon in the following reaction:

    $2Fe_2O_3 + 3C \rightarrow 4Fe + 3CO_2$

    02.2 Calculate the relative formula mass (M_r) of carbon dioxide (CO_2).

         Relative atomic masses (A_r): carbon = 12; oxygen = 16

         Answer: .... **[1 mark]**

    02.3 Both oxidation and reduction take place when iron is extracted from iron(III) oxide.

         Draw **one** line from each type of change to the name of the substance that is changed in that way.

Change		Substance
		iron
oxidation		iron(III) oxide
		carbon
reduction		carbon dioxide **[2 marks]**

02.4 Gold does not have to undergo an extraction process.

Explain why.

....

....

....

.... **[2 marks]**

03 **Table 1** shows some of the properties of elements in Group 7 of the periodic table.

Table 1

Element	Density (g/cm³)	Melting Point (°C)	Boiling Point (°C)
Fluorine	0.0017	−219.6	−188.1
Chlorine	0.0032	−101.5	−34.0
Bromine	3.1028	−7.3	58.8
Iodine	4.9330	113.7	184.3

03.1 State **one** trend in the properties of the Group 7 elements as shown in **Table 1**.

....

.... **[1 mark]**

03.2 Astatine is found in Group 7, below iodine.

Use the information in **Table 1** to estimate the melting point of astatine.

Answer: .... °C   **[1 mark]**

Question 3 continues on the next page

03.3 Chlorine and fluorine are both gases at room temperature.

Describe how cooling a mixture of the gases could be used to separate them.

_____

_____

_____

_____ **[3 marks]**

Group 7 elements all exist as molecules containing two atoms.

03.4 Complete the dot and cross diagram in **Figure 2** to show the covalent bonding in a molecule of chlorine.

Show the outer shell electrons only.

Figure 2

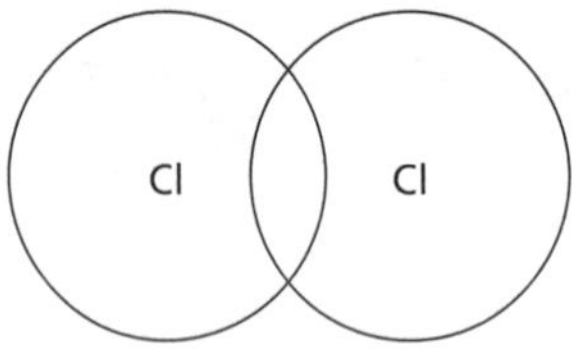

[2 marks]

03.5 What is the formula for a molecule of bromine?

Answer: _____ **[1 mark]**

03.6 Which statement correctly describes what happens when a Group 7 element boils?

Tick **one** box.

Covalent bonds form ☐

Intermolecular forces form ☐

Covalent bonds break ☐

Intermolecular forces break ☐ **[1 mark]**

03.7 The Group 7 elements all react with Group 1 elements to form ionic compounds.

Explain why all the Group 7 elements share this chemical property.

_____

_____ **[1 mark]**

03.8 The Group 1 element sodium reacts with chlorine to form sodium chloride.
Figure 3 shows the outer electrons in an atom of sodium and in an atom of chlorine.

Figure 3

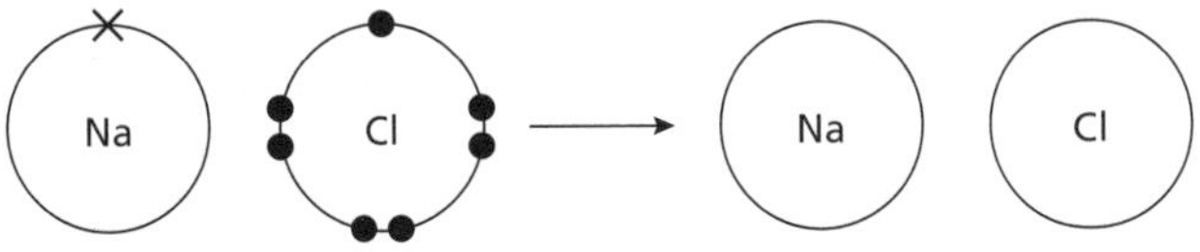

Complete the diagram to show the arrangement of electrons in sodium chloride.
You should give the formula of each ion formed. **[5 marks]**

03.9 The Group 7 elements become less reactive as you go down the group.

Explain why.

_____

_____

_____

_____

_____

_____ **[4 marks]**

Turn over for the next question

04 A student was asked to produce copper(II) sulfate crystals.
They used the method shown in **Figure 4**.

Figure 4

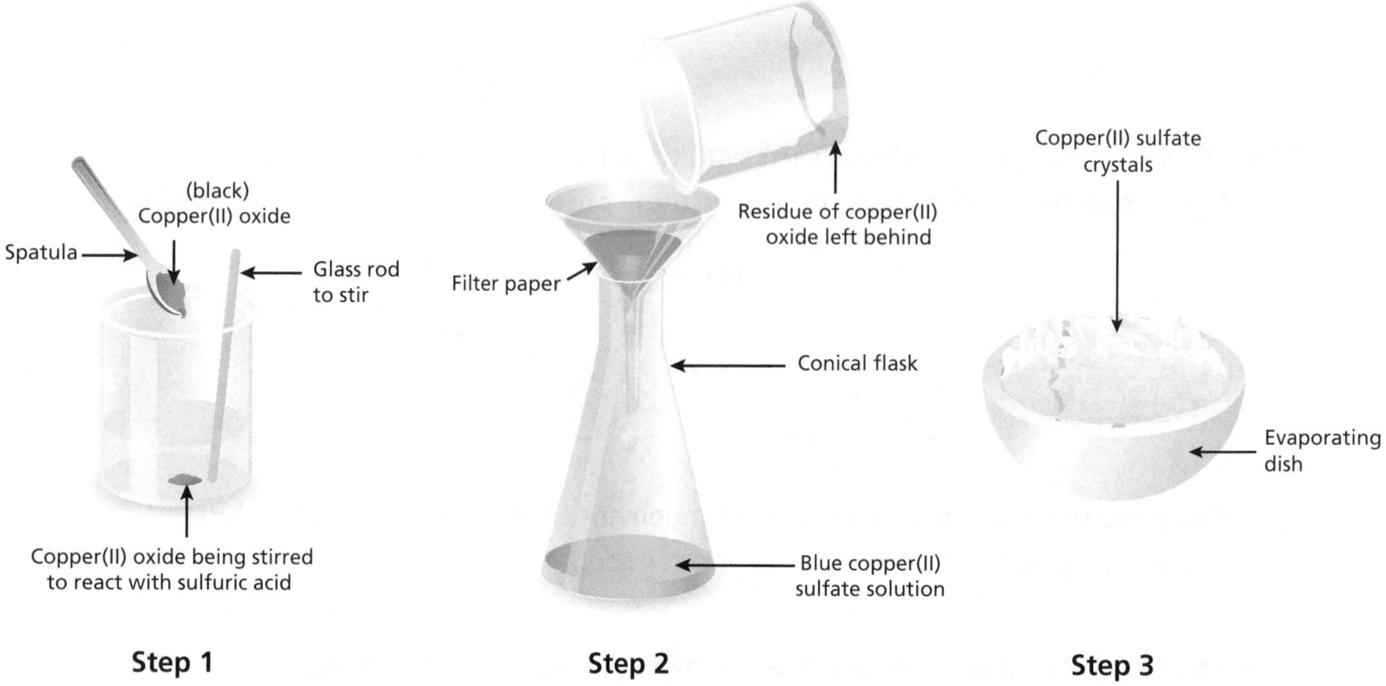

Step 1 labels: Spatula, (black) Copper(II) oxide, Glass rod to stir, Copper(II) oxide being stirred to react with sulfuric acid

Step 2 labels: Filter paper, Residue of copper(II) oxide left behind, Conical flask, Blue copper(II) sulfate solution

Step 3 labels: Copper(II) sulfate crystals, Evaporating dish

Step 1   **Step 2**   **Step 3**

04.1 Give the name of the separation process used in **Step 2** and explain why it was used.

....

....

....

.... **[2 marks]**

04.2 Identify one hazard in **Step 1** or **Step 2** and suggest a method of reducing the risk.

Hazard: ....

Way of reducing the risk: ....

.... **[2 marks]**

The equation for the reaction is:

$CuO(s) + H_2SO_4(aq) \rightarrow CuSO_4.5H_2O\ (aq) + H_2O(l)$

04.3 The student used 5.2 g of copper(II) oxide.

Calculate the theoretical yield of copper(II) sulfate crystals ($CuSO_4.5H_2O$).

Relative atomic masses (A_r): H = 1; C = 12; O = 16; S = 32; Cu = 63.5

Answer: .... **g**   **[4 marks]**

04.4 The student produced less copper(II) sulfate than the theoretical yield.

Suggest **one** reason why.

....

....   **[1 mark]**

04.5 Look at the two equations:

$CuO(s) + H_2SO_4(aq) \rightarrow CuSO_4.5H_2O(aq) + H_2O(l)$

$Cu(OH)_2(s) + H_2SO_4(aq) \rightarrow CuSO_4.5H_2O(aq) + 2H_2O(l)$

Compare the atom economies of the two reactions for making copper(II) sulfate.
You are **not** expected to calculate the atom economies of either reaction.
Give a reason for the difference.

....

....

....   **[2 marks]**

Turn over for the next question

05   **Figure 5** shows the structure of graphite.

Figure 5

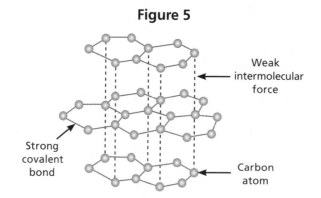

05.1 Graphite and diamond are both giant covalent compounds.

State **one difference** and **one similarity** between the structures of
diamond and graphite.

Similarity: ....

....

Difference: ....

.... **[2 marks]**

05.2 Graphene is a single layer of graphite.
Its properties include being an electrical conductor, strong and transparent.
In the future, it could be used to make touch-screens for electronic devices like
mobile phones.

Explain why graphene has these properties in terms of its structure and
why it is a good choice of material for a touch-screen.

....

....

....

....

....

....

....

[6 marks]

06 A student was asked to carry out the electrolysis of copper(II) sulfate solution using inert graphite electrodes.

06.1 Complete **Figure 6** to show the apparatus they should use.
Label the following on your completed diagram:
- Anode
- Cathode.

Figure 6

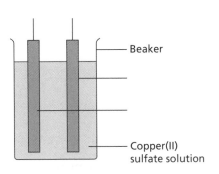

Beaker

Copper(II)
sulfate solution

[3 marks]

06.2 Hydrogen (H^+) ions and copper (Cu^{2+}) ions are both attracted to the cathode but only one product is formed.

Predict the name of the product formed at the cathode.
Explain why only this product is formed.

....

.... [2 marks]

06.3 Complete the balanced half equation for the reaction at the anode.

$4OH^-(aq) \rightarrow$ .... $H_2O(l) + O_2(g) +$ .... e^- [2 marks]

06.4 Is the reaction at the anode an example of reduction or oxidation?
Give a reason for your answer.

....

....

.... [2 marks]

Turn over for the next question

07 Hydrochloric acid neutralises sodium hydroxide solution.
The equation for the reaction is:

$HCl(aq) + NaOH(aq) \rightarrow NaCl(aq) + H_2O(l)$

07.1 Calculate the mass of sodium hydroxide that needs to be added to 1 dm³ of water to form a solution of concentration 0.100 mol/dm³.

Relative atomic masses (A_r): H = 1; O = 16; Na = 23

Answer: _____ **g** **[3 marks]**

A student is asked to use a titration to find out the volume of 0.100 mol/dm³ hydrochloric acid needed to neutralise 25 cm³ of 0.100 mol/dm³ sodium hydroxide.

The student places 25 cm³ of sodium hydroxide into a conical flask.
They put a white tile underneath the conical flask.

07.2 Describe how the student would complete the titration.
You should name a suitable indicator and state the colour change that would take place.

_____

_____

_____

_____

_____

[4 marks]

07.3 What is the function of the white tile?

....

.... **[2 marks]**

07.4 The student carries out the titration.
They measure the volume of hydrochloric acid needed to neutralise the sodium hydroxide as 19.1 cm³.

Describe how the student could reduce the errors in their results.

....

....

....

.... **[2 marks]**

Another student repeated the titration but added the hydrochloric acid to the sodium hydroxide 2.5 cm³ at a time.
They measured the change in pH of the mixture using a pH probe.

Figure 7 shows the graph of their results with a line of best fit plotted.

Figure 7

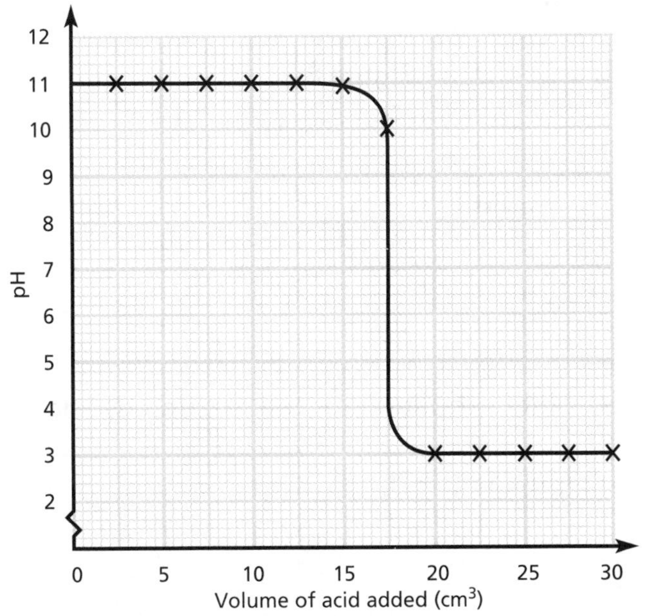

Question 7 continues on the next page

07.5 State the volume of sodium hydroxide needed to neutralise the acid.

Answer: _____ cm³   **[1 mark]**

07.6 What else could the student do to be more certain of the volume needed?

....

....

....   **[2 marks]**

07.7 By what factor did the hydrogen ion concentration change during the titration?

Tick **one** box.

10   ☐

100   ☐

1 000 000   ☐

100 000 000   ☐   **[1 mark]**

08 A student investigated how the mass of magnesium changes when it reacts with dilute hydrochloric acid.

Figure 8 shows the apparatus they used.

Figure 8

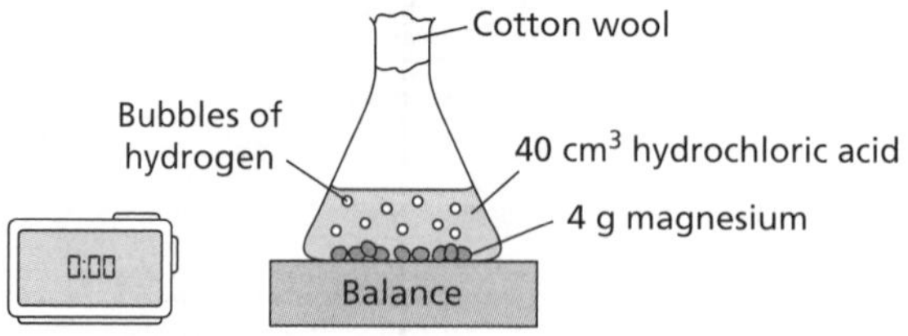

08.1 Complete the balanced symbol equation for the reaction by adding state symbols.

Mg .... $+ 2HCl$ .... $\rightarrow MgCl_2(aq) + H_2$ ....   **[1 mark]**

08.2 State **one** function of the cotton wool.

....

.... **[1 mark]**

Table 2 shows the student's results.

Table 2

Time in s	Total loss of mass in g
0	0.00
10	1.25
20	2.30
30	3.00
40	3.45
50	3.70
60	3.87
70	4.00
80	4.00
90	4.00

08.3 On **Figure 9**:
- Plot the results from **Table 2**.
- Draw a line of best fit.

Figure 9

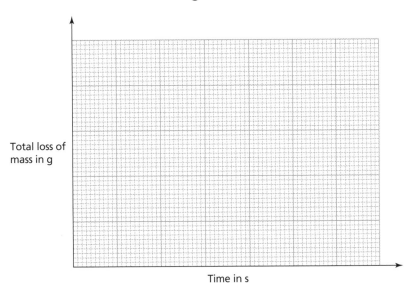

Total loss of mass in g

Time in s

[4 marks]

Question 8 continues on the next page

08.4 At what time did the mass loss stop changing?

Answer: _____ s **[1 mark]**

08.5 The student observed that there was still magnesium in the flask at this time.

Explain why the mass loss stopped changing.

_____

_____ **[1 mark]**

08.6 Explain, in terms of particles, why the mass changes during the reaction.

_____

_____

_____

_____ **[2 marks]**

08.7 Zinc is less reactive than magnesium.

Sketch a line on the graph in **Figure 9** to show the results you would expect if the experiment was repeated using zinc of the same surface area.

Label this line A. **[2 marks]**

09 This question is about the reaction of hydrogen with oxygen.
The equation for the reaction is:

$2H_2(g) + O_2(g) \rightarrow 2H_2O(g)$

It takes place when hydrogen is burned during combustion and also in fuel cells.

09.1 Calculate the volume of gaseous water (steam) produced at room temperature and pressure if 3.5 g of hydrogen is burned.

Relative atomic masses (A_r): H = 1; O = 16

Answer: _____ dm³ **[3 marks]**

Figure 10 shows the displayed formulae for the reaction of hydrogen with oxygen.

Figure 10

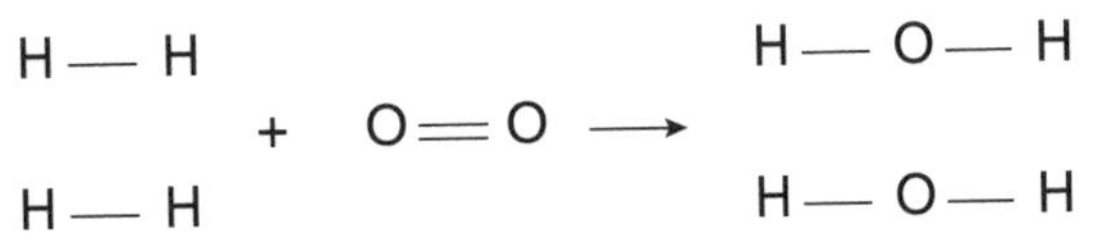

H — H
                    +   O ═ O   ⟶   H — O — H
H — H   H — O — H

The bond enthalpies for the reaction are shown in **Table 3**.

Table 3

	H–H	O=O	O–H
Energy (kJ/mol)	432	495	467

09.2 Calculate the energy transferred in the reaction.

Answer: _____ kJ/mol **[3 marks]**

Question 9 continues on the next page

09.3 Explain, in terms of bond energies, why the reaction is exothermic.

[2 marks]

09.4 In a fuel cell, hydrogen is oxidised to produce a potential difference.

Complete the half equation which shows what happens at the cathode.

$2H_2 \rightarrow$ _____ [2 marks]

09.5 Electric cars can be powered by hydrogen fuel cells or a rechargeable battery.

Evaluate the use of fuel cells instead of a rechargeable battery.

[4 marks]

END OF QUESTIONS

Collins

GCSE
CHEMISTRY
Paper 2 Higher tier

Materials

Time allowed: 1 hour 45 minutes

For this paper you must have:

- a ruler
- a calculator
- the periodic table (see page 72).

Instructions

- Answer **all** questions in the spaces provided.
- Do all rough work on the page. Cross through any work you do not want to be marked.

Information

- There are **100** marks available on this paper.
- The marks for each question are shown in brackets.
- You are expected to use a calculator where appropriate.
- You are reminded of the need for good English and clear presentation in your answers.

Advice

- In all calculations, show clearly how you work out your answer.

01   This question is about atmospheric pollutants from fuels.

Methane (CH_4) is a hydrocarbon which is used as a fuel.

The equation shows the reaction for the complete combustion of methane:

$$CH_4 + 2O_2 \rightarrow CO_2 + XH_2O$$

01.1 X represents what number?

Tick **one** box.

1   ☐

2   ☐

3   ☐

4   ☐   **[1 mark]**

If there is a limited amount of oxygen then methane will undergo incomplete combustion.
One product is carbon monoxide.

01.2 Which other product may be produced in this reaction?

Tick **one** box.

carbon particles   ☐

sulfur dioxide   ☐

nitrogen oxide   ☐

hydrogen   ☐   **[1 mark]**

01.3 Explain why carbon monoxide is a toxic gas.

....

....

....   **[2 marks]**

01.4 When methane is burned at high temperatures, oxides of nitrogen are produced by the reaction between nitrogen and oxygen from the air.

Which equation correctly shows the production of nitrogen dioxide?

Tick **one** box.

$N + O_2 \rightarrow NO_2$ ☐

$2N_2 + O_2 \rightarrow 2N_2O$ ☐

$N + O \rightarrow NO$ ☐

$N_2 + 2O_2 \rightarrow 2NO_2$ ☐

[1 mark]

01.5 Increased amounts of pollutants in the air cause problems.

Draw **one** line from each pollutant to the problem it causes.

Pollutant		Problem
		global warming
sulfur dioxide		global dimming
		acid rain
carbon particles		destruction of ozone layer

[2 marks]

Turn over for the next question

02   **Figure 1** shows the apparatus that a student used to investigate the rusting of iron.

This is the method they used for each test tube:

1. Measure the mass of the nail.
2. Leave the nail in the test tube for six days.
3. Measure the mass of the nail after six days.

Figure 1

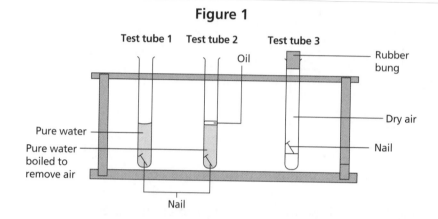

Table 1 shows the student's measurements.

Table 1

Test tube	Mass of nail (g)	Mass of nail after 6 days (g)
1	6.25	6.61
2	6.34	6.34
3	6.32	6.32

02.1 The student used a paper towel to dry the nails before measuring their mass after six days.

Why did the student do this?

_____ **[1 mark]**

02.2 Calculate the change in mass for the nail in Test tube 1.

Answer: _____ **g** **[1 mark]**

02.3 The student's conclusion was that both air and water are required for rusting.

Explain how the results support this conclusion.

....

....

....

....

.... **[4 marks]**

Rust is hydrated iron(III) oxide.
The word equation for the reaction is:

iron + oxygen + water → hydrated iron(III) oxide

Adding salt (sodium chloride) to water speeds up rusting.

02.4 Why is salt not shown in the word equation?

.... **[1 mark]**

02.5 Predict how adding salt to the water in Test tube 1 would affect the change in mass after six days.

Give a reason for your answer.

....

....

.... **[2 marks]**

02.6 Explain how sacrificial protection can be used to stop steel ships from rusting.

....

....

....

....

.... **[3 marks]**

Turn over for the next question

03 Cracking can be carried out in the laboratory using the apparatus shown in **Figure 2**.

Figure 2

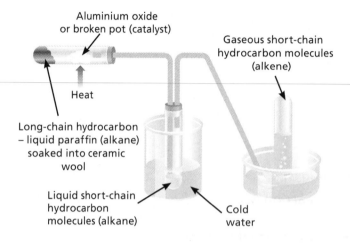

One example of a cracking reaction is:

$C_{10}H_{22} \rightarrow C_7H_{16} + \textbf{M}$

03.1 State the formula and name of **M**.

Formula: ....

Name: .... **[2 marks]**

03.2 Describe a test to show that the gas produced is an alkene.

Give the expected result of the test.

....

....

.... **[2 marks]**

03.3 Alkenes can be used to make polymers.

Complete the equation to show the structure of poly(ethene).

n H₂C=CH₂ →

$$n \quad \begin{matrix} H & & H \\ & \diagdown & \diagup \\ & C = C \\ & \diagup & \diagdown \\ H & & H \end{matrix} \quad \longrightarrow$$

[2 marks]

There are two types of poly(ethene): low density (LD) and high density (HD).
The type of poly(ethene) made is determined by the conditions used during the
polymerisation reaction.

Table 2 shows the properties of the two types of poly(ethene).

Table 2

Property	LD Poly(ethene)	HD Poly(ethene)
Density	0.91–0.94 g/cm³	0.95–0.97 g/cm³
Flexibility	High	Low
Strength	Low	High

03.4 State **one** condition that affects the type of poly(ethene) produced during the
polymerisation reaction.

_____ [1 mark]

03.5 A manufacturer wants to make plastic buckets.

Suggest what type of poly(ethene) they should use.
Give a reason for your choice.

_____

_____

_____ [2 marks]

Turn over for the next question

04 An increase in average global temperature is a cause of climate change.

Explain the effects of global climate change on the environment, humans and wildlife.

....

....

....

....

....

....

....

....

....

....

....

....

....

....

[6 marks]

05 Carbon and other elements are added to iron to make the alloy steel.

Figure 3 shows how the amount of carbon added to iron affects the properties of steel.

Figure 3

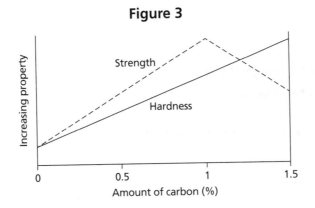

05.1 Describe what happens to the hardness and strength of steel as the amount of carbon is increased.

....

....

....

.... **[3 marks]**

05.2 Cutting tools are usually made from high-carbon steel (>1% carbon).

Give **one** advantage and **one** disadvantage of using high-carbon steel to make cutting tools.

....

....

.... **[2 marks]**

05.3 A piece of steel with a mass of 25 g contains 3 g of chromium.

Calculate the percentage of chromium in the steel.

Answer: .... % **[2 marks]**

Question 5 continues on the next page

05.4 Why is chromium added to steel?

....

.... **[1 mark]**

05.5 Steel and aluminium are used to make drinks cans.
They are both limited resources.

Explain what is meant by 'limited resources'.

....

.... **[1 mark]**

05.6 The metal from drinks cans can be recycled.

The following steps are used:
1. The cans are collected and sorted.
2. They are melted down and then cooled to form blocks of metal.
3. The blocks are rolled into thin sheets, which can be used to make new products.

Evaluate the use of recycling metal cans as a method of reducing the use of limited resources.

....

....

....

....

....

....

.... **[5 marks]**

06 Magnesium reacts with dilute hydrochloric acid:

$Mg(s) + 2HCl(aq) \rightarrow MgCl_2(aq) + H_2(g)$

A student investigated how the volume of hydrogen produced over time changes when magnesium is reacted with two different concentrations of dilute hydrochloric acid.

This is the method used:
1. Measure 20 cm³ of 0.5 mol/dm³ hydrochloric acid using a measuring cylinder.
2. Pour the acid into the conical flask.
3. Add 2 g of magnesium strip.
4. Place the bung into the flask.
5. Measure the volume of gas every 30 seconds until the reaction is complete.
6. Repeat using 1 mol/dm³ hydrochloric acid.

The student reached the end of Step 2 and set up the apparatus as shown in **Figure 4**.

Figure 4

06.1 Identify what the student should do before continuing with the method.
Describe what could happen if the student continued without making any changes.
Explain how this would affect the results.

_____

_____

_____

_____

[3 marks]

Question 6 continues on the next page

The student corrected the error.

Their results are shown in **Table 3**.

Table 3

Time in s	Total volume of hydrogen in cm³	
	0.5 mol/dm³ acid	1 mol/dm³ acid
0	0.0	0.0
30	8.2	14.1
60	14.4	25.5
90	20.0	33.6
120	25.1	36.8
150	29.3	37.6
180	33.7	38.0
210	36.2	38.0
240	37.8	38.0
270	38.0	38.0

06.2 On **Figure 5**:

- Plot both sets of results on the grid.
- Draw two lines of best fit.

Figure 5

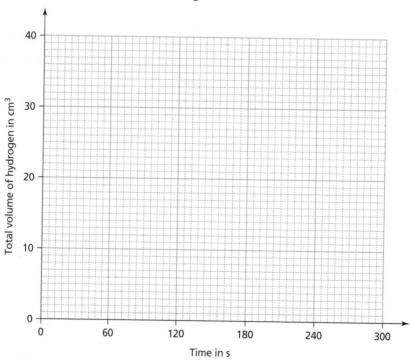

[4 marks]

06.3 How does the concentration of acid affect the rate of the reaction?

....

.... [1 mark]

06.4 Explain why, in terms of particles, the concentration of acid affects the rate of
the reaction.

....

....

....

....

.... [3 marks]

The student decided to research how the temperature of the acid affected the rate of reaction.

Figure 6 shows a graph the student found in a text book.

Figure 6

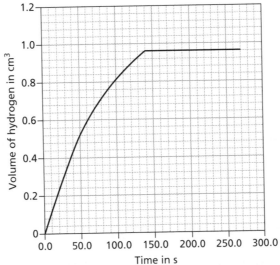

06.5 State the time at which the reaction finishes.

Answer: .... s [1 mark]

Question 6 continues on the next page

06.6 Use **Figure 6** to calculate the rate of the reaction at 50 seconds.
Give your answer to one significant figure.
Give the unit.

Rate of reaction = _____ **[6 marks]**

07 This question is about how the amounts of the different gases in the atmosphere have changed.

Figure 7 shows how the levels of oxygen in the atmosphere have changed since the Earth was formed.

Figure 7

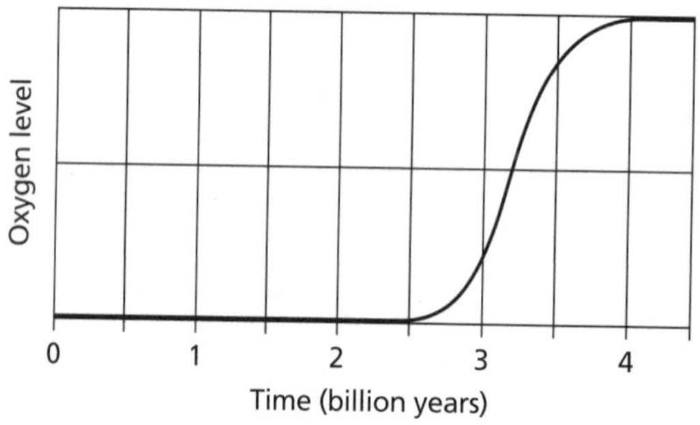

07.1 Use the graph to state when oxygen first started to be produced.

Answer: _____ billion years **[1 mark]**

07.2 The air today is approximately one-fifth oxygen.

Calculate the approximate volume of oxygen in 200 cm³ of air.

Answer: _____ cm³ **[1 mark]**

07.3 Explain how the amount of oxygen in the air increased to the amount found today.

....

....

....

....

....

....

[3 marks]

Another gas found in the air today is carbon dioxide.

07.4 Describe how carbon dioxide helps to maintain temperatures on Earth.

....

....

....

....

....

[3 marks]

07.5 In what way has the amount of carbon dioxide in the atmosphere changed over the last 100 years?

[1 mark]

....

07.6 Describe **one** way in which human activity has brought about this change to the amount of carbon dioxide in the atmosphere today.

....

[2 marks]

....

Turn over for the next question

08 A student carried out a series of chemical tests to identify the ions present in an unknown solution.

The student carried out a flame test.
The flame produced was yellow.

08.1 Identify the metal ion present.

.... **[1 mark]**

08.2 Explain why flame emission spectroscopy is more accurate at identifying the metal ions present in a solution.

....

....

.... **[2 marks]**

The student also carried out the tests shown in **Table 4**.

Table 4

Test	Observation
Add dilute hydrochloric acid	Fizzing
Add silver nitrate solution in the presence of dilute nitric acid	No change
Add barium chloride solution in the presence of hydrochloric acid	White precipitate formed

08.3 What conclusions can be made from these observations?

....

....

....

.... **[3 marks]**

Paper chromatography can also be used to identify substances.

Figure 8 shows the results from chromatography carried out on a mixture.

Figure 8

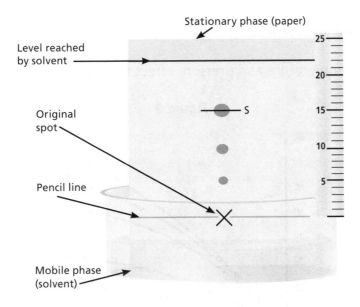

08.4 How many substances are present in the mixture?

Answer: _____ [1 mark]

08.5 To identify a substance its R_f value must be calculated.

Calculate the R_f value of **S**.
Give your answer to 2 decimal places.

Answer: _____ [3 marks]

08.6 Explain how paper chromatography separates the substances in a mixture.

_____

_____

_____ [3 marks]

Turn over for the next question

09   Ammonia is used to produce nitrogen-based fertilisers.

The Haber process is used to manufacture ammonia.

The equation for the reaction is:

nitrogen + hydrogen $\rightleftharpoons$ ammonia

The forward reaction is exothermic.

Figure 9 shows how temperature and pressure affect the amount of ammonia produced.

Figure 9

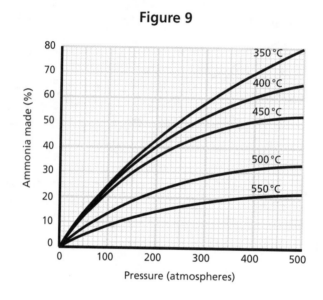

09.1 State the pressure and temperature that result in the highest yield of ammonia.

Pressure: .... **atmospheres**   **[1 mark]**

Temperature: .... **°C**   **[1 mark]**

09.2 Use Le Chatelier's principle to explain why a low temperature results in a high yield of ammonia.

....

....

....

   [2 marks]

09.3 In reality, a temperature of 450 °C is used.

Explain why.

....

....

....

....

....

.... [3 marks]

09.4 Compounds of potassium and phosphorus are also used as fertilisers.
Potassium compounds and phosphate rock can be mined from the ground.
Potassium compounds such as potassium chloride can be used directly as fertilisers, but
phosphate rock cannot.

Explain why.

....

....

....

....

....

.... [3 marks]

END OF QUESTIONS

The Periodic Table

Group 1	Group 2											Group 3	Group 4	Group 5	Group 6	Group 7	Group 0
																	4 **He** helium 2
7 **Li** lithium 3	9 **Be** beryllium 4											11 **B** boron 5	12 **C** carbon 6	14 **N** nitrogen 7	16 **O** oxygen 8	19 **F** fluorine 9	20 **Ne** neon 10
23 **Na** sodium 11	24 **Mg** magnesium 12											27 **Al** aluminum 13	28 **Si** silicon 14	31 **P** phosphorus 15	32 **S** sulfur 16	35.5 **Cl** chlorine 17	40 **Ar** argon 18
39 **K** potassium 19	40 **Ca** calcium 20	45 **Sc** scandium 21	48 **Ti** titanium 22	51 **V** vanadium 23	52 **Cr** chromium 24	55 **Mn** manganese 25	56 **Fe** iron 26	59 **Co** cobalt 27	59 **Ni** nickel 28	63.5 **Cu** copper 29	65 **Zn** zinc 30	70 **Ga** gallium 31	73 **Ge** germanium 32	75 **As** arsenic 33	79 **Se** selenium 34	80 **Br** bromine 35	84 **Kr** krypton 36
85 **Rb** rubidium 37	88 **Sr** strontium 38	89 **Y** yttrium 39	91 **Zr** zirconium 40	93 **Nb** niobium 41	96 **Mo** molybdenum 42	[98] **Tc** technetium 43	101 **Ru** ruthenium 44	103 **Rh** rhodium 45	106 **Pd** palladium 46	108 **Ag** silver 47	112 **Cd** cadmium 48	115 **In** indium 49	119 **Sn** tin 50	122 **Sb** antimony 51	128 **Te** tellurium 52	127 **I** iodine 53	131 **Xe** xenon 54
133 **Cs** caesium 55	137 **Ba** barium 56	139 **La*** lanthanum 57	178 **Hf** hafnium 72	181 **Ta** tantalum 73	184 **W** tungsten 74	186 **Re** rhenium 75	190 **Os** osmium 76	192 **Ir** iridium 77	195 **Pt** platinum 78	197 **Au** gold 79	201 **Hg** mercury 80	204 **Tl** thallium 81	207 **Pb** lead 82	209 **Bi** bismuth 83	[209] **Po** polonium 84	[210] **At** astatine 85	[222] **Rn** radon 86
[223] **Fr** francium 87	[226] **Ra** radium 88	[227] **Ac*** actinium 89	[261] **Rf** rutherfordium 104	[262] **Db** dubnium 105	[266] **Sg** seaborgium 106	[264] **Bh** bohrium 107	[277] **Hs** hassium 108	[268] **Mt** meitnerium 109	[271] **Ds** darmstadtium 110	[272] **Rg** roentgenium 111	[285] **Cn** copernicium 112	[286] **Uut** ununtrium 113	[289] **Fl** flerovium 114	[289] **Uup** ununpentium 115	[293] **Lv** livermorium 116	[294] **Uus** ununseptium 117	[294] **Uuo** ununoctium 118

1 **H** hydrogen 1

Key

relative atomic mass
atomic symbol
name
atomic (proton) number

* The Lanthanides (atomic numbers 58–71) and the Actinides (atomic numbers 90–103) have been omitted. Relative atomic masses for **Cu** and **Cl** have not been rounded to the nearest whole number.

Answers

Topic-Based Questions

Page 4 Atoms, Elements, Compounds and Mixtures

1. a) $2Cu + O_2 \rightarrow 2CuO$ **[1]**
    b) $18.9 - 15.6 = 3.3g$ **[1]**
    c) 0.1g **[1]**

> The resolution of the balance is the degree of accuracy. In this case, the measurements are given to the nearest 0.1g.

2. a) Place the salt solution in the round bottomed flask **[1]**; heat the solution **[1]**; and collect the liquid that distils at 100°C **[1]**
    b) **Any one of:** Burns from the Bunsen burner / hot water / steam **[1]**; equipment may crack so risk of cuts **[1]**

Page 5 Atoms and the Periodic Table

1. a) Thompson showed that the atom could be divided up into simpler substances **[1]**; the old model was no longer correct **[1]**
    b) Electron **[1]**
2. a) Based on Thompson's model, the alpha particles would have all gone through **[1]** OR There would have been no deflection **[1]** (Accept: It went against Thompson's model)
    b) To reduce the effects of errors **[1]**; to check repeatability **[1]** (Accept: To make sure they were correct / accurate **[1]**)
    c) **Any three of:** small nucleus **[1]**; nucleus in the centre of the atom **[1]**; nucleus has a positive charge **[1]**; electrons in orbit around the nucleus **[1]** (Accept a labelled diagram)

Page 6 The Periodic Table

1. C **[1]**

> The number of electrons in the outer shell is the same as the group that the element is in. The number of electron shells is the same as the row (period) that the element is in.

2. a) X **[1]**; because it does not conduct electricity **[1]**
    b) W **[1]**; because it is a liquid at room temperature **[1]**; and it conducts electricity **[1]**
    c) **Any two of:** Group 1 metals have a lower density **[1]**; lower melting point **[1]**; lower boiling point **[1]**; are softer **[1]**; are less strong / hard-wearing **[1]**; **Plus:** Group 1 metals are more reactive / react more vigorously than transition metals **[1]** (Accept a comparison of a suitable reaction)

Page 7 States of Matter

1. a) g **[1]**; s **[1]**

> Gas = g, solid = s, liquid = l, aqueous / dissolved in water = aq

    b) 650 **[1]**
    c) −183 **[1]**
    d) **Any six of:** Oxygen has a low boiling point **[1]**; magnesium oxide has a high boiling point **[1]**; oxygen has weak forces of attraction between its particles / molecules **[1]**; magnesium has strong forces in between its ions / particles **[1]**; oxygen is a simple molecule **[1]**; magnesium oxide is an ionic compound **[1]**; only a small amount of energy is needed to boil oxygen / turn it from a liquid into a gas **[1]**; a lot of energy is needed to boil magnesium oxide / turn it from a liquid into a gas **[1]**

Page 8 Ionic Compounds

1. a) calcium chloride **[1]**; sodium carbonate **[1]**

> Ionic compounds contain both metal and non-metal elements. Look at the periodic table if you are not sure whether an element is a metal or a non-metal. The metals are on the left side, the non-metals on the right.

    b) They cannot conduct electricity when solid because the ions cannot move **[1]**; they can conduct electricity when in solution because the ions are free to move about **[1]**; and carry the charge **[1]**
2. Electrons are transferred from magnesium to bromine **[1]**; the magnesium atom loses two electrons **[1]**; forming Mg^{2+} / 2+ ions **[1]**; the two bromine atoms each gain one electron **[1]**; forming Br^- / 1− ions **[1]**

Page 9 Metals

1. High melting point: strong force of attraction between positive ions and negative electrons / metallic bond is strong **[1]**; so, a lot of energy is needed to break metallic bonds (to melt metal) **[1]**; thermal conductivity: electrons are delocalised **[1]**; and are free to move through the metal and transfer energy **[1]**; malleability: the ions are arranged in layers / have a regular arrangement **[1]**; the layers are able to slide over each other easily **[1]**

Page 10 Covalent Compounds

1. The forces between bromine molecules are stronger **[1]**

2. a) A shared pair of electrons drawn between H and Br **[1]**; no additional hydrogen electrons and three non-bonding pairs shown on bromine **[1]** (second mark dependent on first)
    b) HBr **[1]**
3. High melting point – Strong covalent bonds between many carbon atoms **[1]**; Does not conduct electricity when molten – There are no charged particles that are free to move **[1]**

> The covalent bonds between atoms are very strong. The force of attraction between molecules is called the intermolecular force and is much weaker.

Page 11 Special Materials

1. a) two / 10^2 **[1]**
    b) Higher surface area to volume ratio **[1]**; better skin coverage **[1]**; higher protection against UV **[1]**
2. a) $5.5 \times 10^{-8}m$ **[1]**
    b) No **[1]**; because the average diameter of the particles is 55nm / between 1 and 100nm **[1]**
3. **Any three of:** Need to know the effects of nanoparticles in the blood at this concentration **[1]**; need to find out the long-term risk of using sun cream **[1]**; the study needs to be repeated by other scientists **[1]**; need to check if the study was biased, e.g. carried out by a sun cream manufacturer **[1]**; need to repeat using more volunteers **[1]**; need to repeat using a wider range of people of different ages / sex / skin type **[1]**

Page 12 Conservation of Mass

1. a) $Zn(s) + 2H^+(aq) \rightarrow Zn^{2+}(aq) + H_2(g)$ **[1]**

> In an ionic equation, only the ions that change (gain or lose electrons) are shown. They must be balanced.

    b) Gas is produced in the flask (increasing the pressure inside) **[1]**; the flask may crack / the bung may be forced out **[1]** (Accept: 'it is not safe' for 1 mark)
    c) The mass reading will decrease **[1]**; because the hydrogen particles (atoms) in the hydrochloric acid are rearranged **[1]**; to form hydrogen gas, which leaves the flask into the air **[1]**

Page 13 Amount of Substance

1. a) $2 \times 2 \times 2 = 8cm^3$ **[1]**
    b) mass = density × volume **[1]**; $10.49 \times 8 = 83.92g$ **[1]**

c) moles = $\frac{mass}{A_r}$ [1]; $\frac{83.92}{108}$ = 0.78 moles [1]

d) 0.5mol of oxygen (O_2) [1]; 12g of carbon (C) [1]

Page 14 Titration

1. a) **Any one of:** student did not stop adding the acid when the end-point was reached [1]; they added the acid too quickly (not drop by drop) [1]; they did not swirl the conical flask as they added the acid [1]

b) $\frac{27.15 + 27.05 + 26.95}{3}$ [1]; = 27.05cm³ [1]

c) Moles HCl: $\frac{27.05}{1000} \times 0.1$ = 0.0027 [1]; moles NaOH: 0.0027 [1]; concentration NaOH: $\frac{0.0027}{0.025}$ [1]; = 0.108 [1]; = 0.108mol/dm³ [1]

Page 15 Percentage Yield and Atom Economy

1. a) Moles Mg: $\frac{3.6}{24}$ = 0.15 [1]; M_r MgO: 24 + 16 = 40 [1]; mass MgO = 0.15 × 40 = 6g [1]

b) **Any one of:** reaction did not go to completion [1]; loss of material when transferring [1]; competing reactions [1]

c) All the atoms in the reactants end up in the product [1]

Page 16 Reactivity of Metals

1. a) magnesium [1]; sodium [1]
   b) i) Carbon [1]
      ii) Zinc(II) oxide [1]
2. Oxidation: Zn → Zn^{2+} + 2e⁻ [1]; Reduction: Cu^{2+} + 2e⁻ → Cu [1]

> Remember, OIL RIG: Oxidation Is Loss (of electrons); Reduction Is Gain (of electrons)

Page 17 The pH Scale and Salts

1. 4 [1]
2. a) Add excess copper(II) oxide to acid (accept alternatives, e.g. 'until no more will react') [1]; filter (to remove excess copper(II) oxide) [1]; heat filtrate to evaporate some water or heat to point of crystallisation [1]; leave to cool (so crystals form) [1]

b) **Any one of:** wear apron [1]; use eye protection [1]; tie hair back [1]

c) Copper(II) chloride [1]

Page 18 Electrolysis

1. a) Aluminium is more reactive than carbon [1]

b) 2 [1]; 4 [1]

c) It requires a lot of electricity to melt the aluminium oxide / keep it molten [1]; so aluminium oxide is dissolved in molten cryolite [1]; to reduce the melting point, so less electricity is used [1]

Page 19 Exothermic and Endothermic Reactions

1. a) It reduces the movement of heat to and from the surroundings [1]; which could affect the accuracy of the results [1] (Accept 'it is an insulator' for 1 mark)

b) **Any two of:** type of acid [1]; concentration of acid [1]; surface area of metal [1]; temperature of acid [1]; volume of acid [1]; mass of metal [1]

c) The more reactive the metal [1]; the more exothermic the reaction [1]

Page 20 Fuel Cells

1. a) It would produce no voltage [1]

b) Metal A [1]; because it gives the most negative voltage [1]

c) Use five cells like the one shown in Figure 1 [1]; connected in series [1]

Page 21 Rate of Reaction

1. a) Repeat using different concentrations of acid [1]; for example, 0.5mol/dm³, 1mol/dm³, 1.5mol/dm³, 2mol/dm³ [1] (Accept any other concentrations within a sensible range)

b) **Any one of:** wear eye protection [1]; wear apron [1]; do not heat mixture over 50°C [1]

c) The time taken for the cross to disappear will decrease as concentration of acid increases [1]; as the (acid) concentration increases so does the number of (acid) particles in a given volume [1]; so they collide more often with the sodium thiosulfate particles [1]; resulting in more successful collisions and a reaction taking place (sulfur forming) [1]

Page 22 Reversible Reactions

1. a) Reversible (reaction) [1]

b) Forward reaction [1]; the backward reaction is endothermic [1]; because heat is needed to decompose the ammonium chloride [1]

c) The forward and reverse reactions are taking place at the same rate. [1]; The amounts of reactants and products are constant. [1]

d) More ammonium chloride will be produced [1]; until equilibrium is reached again [1]

Page 23 Alkanes

1. a) A molecule / compound [1]; that only contains carbon and hydrogen [1]

b) The different molecules / hydrocarbons condense [1]; at a place in the column just below their boiling point [1]

2. O_2 [1]; 2 [1]

Page 24 Alkenes

1. a) 2 [1]
   b) C_5H_{10} and C_2H_4 [1]
2. Add bromine water [1]; if it goes colourless it is an alkene [1]; if it stays orange / brown / does not change colour then it is an alkane [1]

Page 25 Organic Compounds

1. a) Circle around the OH group [1]
   b) Ethanol [1]
   c) i) Observation: the universal indicator would turn green [1]; Reason: ethanol has a neutral pH / pH of 7 [1]
      ii) Observation: bubbles / fizzing [1]; Reason: hydrogen is produced [1]
   d) Carboxylic acid [1] (Accept a named example, e.g. ethanoic acid)

Page 26 Polymerisation

1. a) Correct bonds drawn in monomer [1]; five single bonds drawn on polymer (one C–C and four C–H) [1]; two open-ended bonds from carbon atoms [1]

Monomer (propene)   Polymer

b) Poly(propene) [1] (Accept: polypropene)

> To name a polymer, just add 'poly' before the name of the monomer.

2. When heated the weak intermolecular bonds in the thermosoftening polymer will break [1]; so the chains can separate from each other [1]; and move around (to form a liquid) [1]; but the strong cross-links in the thermosetting plastic will not break [1]

Page 27 Chemical Analysis

1. a) Paper [1]
   b) Pencil [1]; the ink from the pen would 'run' on the paper / dissolve in the solvent and affect the results [1]
   c) B and C [1]; there is only one spot [1]
   d) 18cm (distance moved by X) and 28cm (distance moved by solvent) [1]; $\frac{18}{28}$ [1] = 0.64286 = 0.64 to 2 d.p. [1] (award 2 marks if calculation is correct but the answer is not given to 2 d.p.)

Page 28 Identifying Substances

1. a) To clean the (nichrome) wire **[1]**; to remove any other substances that could affect the results of the flame test **[1]**
    b) Sodium chloride **[1]**; The yellow flame test shows the metal ion (cation) is sodium **[1]**; the silver nitrate test produced white silver chloride **[1]**; which shows chloride is present (in the compound) **[1]**
    c) **Any two of:** instrumental tests are more accurate **[1]**; quick (rapid) **[1]**; sensitive **[1]**; useful if only a small sample is available for testing **[1]**

Page 29 The Earth's Atmosphere

1. C **[1]**
2. $\frac{0.05}{4.2} \times 100$ **[1]**; = 1.2% **[1]**
3. a) Evidence **[1]**; that supported their theory **[1]**
    b) **Any three of:** it happened a long time ago **[1]**; nobody was alive to record how it happened **[1]**; there is little evidence available **[1]**; there is evidence to support both theories **[1]**

Page 30 Greenhouse Gases

1. a) Carbon dioxide OR methane **[1]**; **plus:** increased burning of fossil fuels / increased deforestation (for carbon dioxide) OR more animal farming (digestion, waste decomposition) / decomposition of rubbish in landfill sites (for methane) **[1]**
    b) From: 0.6°C **[1]**; To: 3.6°C **[1]** (If no units are included only award 1 mark)
    c) **Any two of:** complex systems **[1]**; many different variables **[1]**; may only be based on parts of evidence **[1]**

Page 31 Earth's Resources

1. a) Water that is safe to drink **[1]**
    b) It contains dissolved substances **[1]**; it is a mixture as it contains more than just water molecules **[1]**
    c) **Any one of:** adding chlorine **[1]**; adding ozone **[1]**; using UV light **[1]**
    d) To remove the water from the salt **[1]**
    e) The sea water needs to be heated **[1]**; which requires a large amount of energy **[1]**

Page 32 Using Resources

1. **Any six of:** wood pulp is from trees, a renewable resource **[1]**; trees should be replanted before wood pulp can be considered a sustainable resource **[1]**; clay, chalk and titanium oxide are quarried which can have negative environmental impacts **[1]**; paper production uses a lot of water **[1]**; transportation of plastic bags uses less fuel **[1]**; plastic is longer lasting / can be reused many times **[1]**; (plastic longer lasting) so plastic may use less finite resources **[1]**; (plastic may use less finite resources) and so plastic may have a lower energy requirement **[1]**; paper is biodegradable so spends less time in landfill **[1]**; paper is more likely to be recycled which lowers raw material usage **[1]**

> For this type of question, the examiner will expect your answer to be given in a clear and logical way, using good English and correct grammar and punctuation. They will award 5–6 marks for a clear description of the advantages and disadvantages of both types of bag, with logical links; 3–4 marks if a number of relevant points are made, but the logic is unclear; 1–2 marks for fragmented points, with no logical structure.

Page 33 The Haber Process

1. a) A catalyst **[1]**; to increase the rate of reaction **[1]**
    b) To prevent it breaking down into hydrogen and nitrogen **[1]**; and increase the yield made in the time **[1]**
2. a) P: phosphorus **[1]**; K: potassium **[1]**
    b) 20×0.24 **[1]**; = 4.8kg **[1]**

Pages 35–52 GCSE Chemistry Practice Exam Paper 1

01.1 Proton +1, Neutron 0, Electron –1 **[1]**
01.2 It has equal numbers of protons and neutrons / equal numbers of positive and negative charges **[1]**
01.3 Mass number 4, Atomic number 2 **[1]**

> The atomic number is the number of protons (and also electrons). The mass number is the total number of particles in the nucleus (protons plus neutrons).

01.4 It has a full outer shell of electrons. **[1]**
01.5 It has the same atomic number **[1]**; It has a different mass number **[1]**
02.1 5 **[1]**
02.2 (12 + 16 + 16) = 44 **[1]**
02.3 oxidation–carbon **[1]**; reduction–iron(III) oxide **[1]**
02.4 It is found pure in the ground **[1]**; because it is unreactive **[1]**
03.1 **Any one of:** the density increases as you go down the group **[1]**; the melting point increases as you go down the group **[1]**; the boiling point increases as you go down the group **[1]** (Accept alternative answers, e.g. the density decreases as you go up the group)

03.2 Any answer in the range 200–230°C **[1]**
03.3 Cool the mixture to –34°C **[1]**; chlorine will become a liquid **[1]**; and can be drained off **[1]**
03.4 One shared pair of electrons drawn between the two atoms **[1]**; three non-bonding pairs drawn on each atom **[1]** (the second mark will only be awarded if the first mark is achieved)

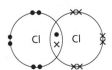

03.5 Br_2 **[1]**
03.6 Intermolecular forces break **[1]**
03.7 They all have the same number of electrons (seven) in their outer shell **[1]**
03.8 Sodium ion has no electrons drawn **[1]**; labelled Na^+ / + ion **[1]**; chlorine ion has eight electrons drawn **[1]**; seven represented by dots and one a cross **[1]**; labelled Cl^- / 1– ion **[1]**

03.9 The atoms get larger **[1]**; the outer shell gets further from the nucleus **[1]**; the attraction between the nucleus and electrons gets weaker **[1]**; so an electron is less easily gained **[1]**
04.1 Filtration **[1]**; to remove the excess copper(II) oxide **[1]**
04.2 Hazard: **any one of:** chemical on skin **[1]**; chemical in eyes **[1]**; cuts from broken glass **[1]**; Way of reducing the risk: **any one of (as appropriate to hazard):** wash hands **[1]**; wear eye protection **[1]**; ask teacher to clear away broken glass **[1]**
04.3 M_r CuO = 63.5 + 16 = 79.5 **[1]**; M_r CuSO₄.5H₂O = 63.5 + 32 + (16 × 4) + 5 × (2 × 1 + 16) = 249.5 **[1]**; moles CuO = $\frac{5.2}{79.5}$ = 0.0654088 **[1]**; mass CuSO₄.5H₂O = 0.0654088 × 249.5 = 16.3g **[1]**
04.4 **Any one of:** reaction did not go to completion **[1]**; loss of material when transferring **[1]**; competing reactions **[1]**
04.5 Atom economy using hydroxide is lower / using oxide is higher **[1]**; because two molecules of water are made compared to one / sum of relative formula masses of reactants is greater for $Cu(OH)_2$ **[1]**
05.1 Similarity: **any one of:** they both are made up of carbon atoms **[1]**; both contain strong covalent bonds between carbon atoms **[1]**

Difference: **any one of:** graphite is made up of layers, diamond has no layers [1]; graphite contains weak intermolecular forces, diamond only contains strong covalent bonds [1]; graphite has delocalised (free) electrons, diamond does not [1]

05.2 Electrical conductivity comes from delocalised electrons, which are able to move through the structure [1]; this is useful for touch-screens, as they need to be able to conduct electricity to work [1]; strength comes from strong covalent bonds between carbon atoms [1]; this is useful for touch-screens so they do not crack / shatter when dropped [1]; graphene is transparent because it is only one atom thick [1]; this is useful for touch-screens so you can see the light coming through from the display underneath [1]

06.1 Battery / cell added and joined to electrodes [1]; electrode connected to positive side of cell labelled anode [1]; electrode connected to negative side of cell labelled cathode [1]

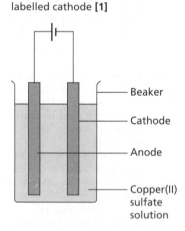

- Beaker
- Cathode
- Anode
- Copper(II) sulfate solution

06.2 Copper [1]; it is less reactive than hydrogen [1]
06.3 2 [1]; 4 [1]
06.4 Oxidation [1]; because electrons are lost from the (hydroxide) ions [1]
07.1 M_r NaOH = 23 + 16 + 1 = 40 [1]; mass of NaOH = 0.100 × 40 [1]; = 4g [1]
07.2 Add indicator, e.g. phenolphthalein / methyl orange / litmus added to the sodium hydroxide (in the conical flask) [1]; add the acid from a burette drop by drop and swirl each time [1]; until the indicator just changes colour [1]; from pink to colourless (for phenolphthalein) / yellow to red (for methyl orange) / blue to red (for litmus) [1]
07.3 To clearly see the end-point [1]; for accurate measurement of volume of acid [1]
07.4 Repeat (the titration) [1]; calculate a mean [1]
07.5 17.5cm³ [1]

07.6 Add the acid in smaller volumes (less than 2.5cm³) [1]; around 15cm³ [1] (accept anything in the range 10–20cm³)
07.7 100 000 000 [1]
08.1 **In order:** (s), (aq), (g) [1]
08.2 To let the gas out / to stop the acid spraying [1]
08.3 Sensible scales, using at least half the grid for the points [1]; all points correct [2]; line of best fit drawn [1]

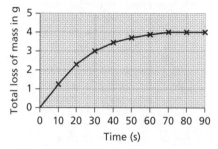

08.4 70s [1]
08.5 All of the acid had reacted [1]
08.6 Hydrogen gas is formed [1]; which escapes into the air [1]
08.7 Less steep line to right of original line [1]; finishes at same overall mass loss [1]
09.1 Moles of $H_2 = \frac{3.5}{2}$ = 1.75 [1]; moles of H_2O = 1.75 [1]; volume of H_2O = 1.75 × 24 = 42dm³ [1]

> One mole of any gas has a volume of 24dm³ at room temperature and pressure.

09.2 Bonds broken = (432 × 2) + 495 = 1359kJ/mol [1]; bonds formed = 467 × 4 = 1868kJ/mol [1]; bonds broken – bonds formed = –509kJ/mol [1]
09.3 Less energy is required to break the bonds in the reactants [1]; than is produced when the bonds are formed in the products [1]
09.4 4H⁺ [1]; + 4e⁻ [1]
09.5 **Any four of:** fuel cells have no moving parts so less likely to break / wear out [1]; they are lightweight and small [1]; electric cars cannot travel far without having to be recharged [1]; hydrogen fuel cells can run a long time between being refilled [1]; cost of hydrogen much higher than electricity [1]; not many places to refill hydrogen [1]

Pages 53–71 GCSE Chemistry Practice Exam Paper 2

01.1 2 [1]
01.2 carbon particles [1]
01.3 Carbon monoxide binds with haemoglobin [1]; reducing the amount of oxygen in the blood [1]
01.4 $N_2 + 2O_2 \rightarrow 2NO_2$ [1]

> *Di*- means two, so nitrogen dioxide contains one nitrogen atom and two oxygen atoms.

01.5 sulfur dioxide–acid rain [1]; carbon particles–global dimming [1]
02.1 To reduce errors / increase accuracy [1]
02.2 (6.61 – 6.25) = 0.36g [1]
02.3 The nail in Test tube 1 was the only one that rusted [1]; it was exposed to both water and air [1]; the nail in Test tube 2 was exposed to water but not air [1]; the nail in Test tube 3 was exposed to air but not water [1]
02.4 It is not a reactant / it does not change in the reaction [1]
02.5 The change in mass would be higher [1]; because the rate of rusting would be faster [1]
02.6 Magnesium blocks attached to the steel [1]; magnesium is more reactive than steel [1]; so magnesium reacts before the steel [1]
03.1 Formula: C_3H_6 [1]; Name: Propene [1]
03.2 Add bromine water [1]; turns orange to colourless [1]
03.3 Five single bonds drawn (one C–C and 4 C–H) [1]; open-ended bonds from carbon atoms [1]

$$\left[\begin{array}{cc} H & H \\ | & | \\ C & C \\ | & | \\ H & H \end{array}\right]_n$$

03.4 **Any one of:** temperature [1]; pressure [1]; catalyst [1]
03.5 HD poly(ethene) [1]; because it is stronger [1]
04 **Effects on the environment: any two of:** melting of ice caps [1]; sea level rise, which may cause flooding and coastal erosion [1]; changes in amount, timing and distribution of rainfall [1]; desertification in some regions [1]; more frequent and severe storms [1]
Effects on people: any two of: flooding of homes [1]; migration of people from affected areas [1]; temperature and water stress [1]; lack of food in some regions [1]
Effects on wildlife: any two of: changes to distribution of species [1]; extinction of some species [1]; temperature and water stress [1]; lack of food in some regions [1]
05.1 Hardness increases as the amount of carbon increases [1]; strength increases between 0 and 1% carbon [1]; and then decreases between 1 and 1.5% carbon [1]
05.2 Advantage: very hard so able to cut through hard materials [1]; Disadvantage: not very strong so may break easily [1]
05.3 $\frac{3}{25} \times 100$ [1]; = 12% [1]

05.4 So it does not rust **[1]** (Do not accept 'to make stainless steel')

05.5 They are finite / non-renewable / may run out **[1]**

05.6 **Any five valid points, e.g.** recycling reduces the amount of metal being mined (metals will last longer) **[1]**; mining, processing metals and recycling all require energy, which mostly comes from the use of finite resources **[1]**; collecting and transporting cans uses petrol / diesel **[1]**; sorting cans and rolling metal blocks requires electrical machinery **[1]**; melting the cans requires a lot of energy **[1]**; overall, recycling consumes less energy than producing new cans **[1]**

06.1 Push the plunger of the syringe down to remove any air in it **[1]**; the plunger may be pushed out before the end of the reaction **[1]**; so volume of gas produced not accurately measured **[1]**

06.2 All points plotted correctly for two sets of data **[2]**; two lines of best fit drawn **[2]**

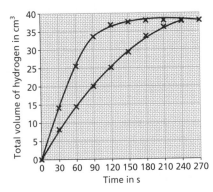

06.3 The higher the concentration, the faster the rate of reaction **[1]**

06.4 As the concentration increases so does the number of particles of acid in a given volume **[1]**; so there are more frequent collisions / more collisions per second with magnesium particles **[1]**; so rate increases / reaction speeds up **[1]**

06.5 140s **[1]**

06.6 Tangent drawn at 50s **[1]**; volume of hydrogen calculated, e.g. 0.62 – 0.28 = 0.34 **[1]**; time calculated, e.g. 70 – 30 = 40 **[1]**; gradient calculated to give rate of reaction, e.g. $\frac{0.34}{40}$ = 0.0085 **[1]**; = 0.009 **[1]**; cm³/s **[1]** (Accept 0.008)

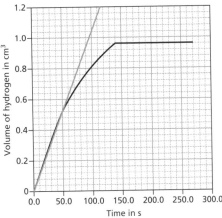

07.1 2.5 billion years **[1]**

07.2 40cm³ **[1]**

07.3 Algae evolved and starting producing oxygen **[1]**; via photosynthesis **[1]**; land plants evolved to increase amounts of oxygen in the atmosphere further **[1]**

07.4 Carbon dioxide allows short wavelength radiation to pass through **[1]**; the atmosphere to the Earth's surface **[1]**; carbon dioxide absorbs outgoing long wavelength radiation **[1]**

07.5 Increased **[1]**

07.6 Increased burning of fossil fuels **[1]**; in vehicle engines/power stations **[1]** OR increased deforestation **[1]**; so fewer trees to absorb carbon dioxide from the air **[1]**

08.1 Sodium **[1]**

08.2 If a sample containing a mixture of ions is used some flame colours can be masked **[1]**; flame emission spectroscopy will identify all metal ions present **[1]**

08.3 It is a mixture **[1]**; containing carbonate ions **[1]**; and sulfate ions **[1]**

08.4 3 **[1]**

08.5 15cm (distance moved by S) and 22cm (distance moved by solvent) **[1]**; $\frac{15}{22}$ = 0.68182 **[1]**; = 0.68 **[1]**

08.6 Mobile phase / solvent moves through the paper **[1]**; and carries different compounds different distances **[1]**; depending on their attraction for the paper and the solvent **[1]**

09.1 Pressure: 500 atmospheres **[1]**; Temperature: 350°C **[1]**

09.2 The reaction is exothermic and so moves to the right **[1]**; because the system moves to increase temperature **[1]**

09.3 To increase the rate of reaction **[1]**; so more ammonia is made in a shorter time **[1]**; to increase profit / amount of money made **[1]**

09.4 Potassium compounds are soluble but phosphate rock is not **[1]**; compounds need to dissolve in water and enter the soil **[1]**; in order to be taken up by plant roots **[1]**

Notes

Notes

Acknowledgements

The author and publisher are grateful to the copyright holders for permission to use quoted materials and images.

Cover and P.1, watchara/Shutterstock.com; Cover and P.1, Everett Historical/Shutterstock.com

Every effort has been made to trace copyright holders and obtain their permission for the use of copyright material. The author and publisher will gladly receive information enabling them to rectify any error or omission in subsequent editions. All facts are correct at time of going to press.

Published by Collins
An imprint of HarperCollinsPublishers Ltd
1 London Bridge Street
London SE1 9GF

© HarperCollinsPublishers Limited 2016

ISBN 9780008326739

Content first published 2016
This edition published 2018

British Library Cataloguing in Publication Data.

A CIP record of this book is available from the British Library.

Commissioning Editor: Emily Linnett and Fiona Burns
Authors: Emma Poole and Gemma Young
Project Manager: Rebecca Skinner
Project Editor: Hannah Dove
Designers: Sarah Duxbury and Paul Oates
Copy-editor: Rebecca Skinner
Technical Readers: John Sadler and Sara Hulse
Proofreader: Tim Jackson
Typesetting and artwork: Jouve India Private Limited
Production: Lyndsey Rogers
Printed by Martins the Printers